Heroin to Hero

Prologue

If you're reading this it means I have agreed to let you see what I've written. If you know me then you won't see me in the same light, and if not you'll hopefully put the light on. Happy and sad, it's all in here.

My life has been a rollercoaster ride so far. Most of the stories you will read here happened when I was still on heroin or during my recovery. Now it is time to share some of the knowledge I have. I wanted to put it all in this book as it may be of importance to someone who feels similar.

I'd love to be able to tell you that it's easy, but I won't lie and that's surely better for us all. Your mindset will dictate your life, so if you want to change for the better then please open your mind up to the possibility of change. That is going to be the only way I can help you to recover. Whether it's gradual or instant it doesn't matter, what matters is your starting to accept that change is needed and that you can do it yourself. Support is out there but it's very scattered at the moment. These charities are working hard to help, but unless we all pull together the problems will never be fixed.

My plan is to donate all the profits from the sale of this book to charity. I will not be corrupted, nor will I lose my way, In the year 2020 we should not have people dying of hypothermia on the streets of Scotland. It snows heavily here at times – what chance do addicts have in those conditions? I will pull the whole country together, sifting through the people who only want financial gain. Charity must be for the cause, not for people to take huge wages. It cannot be justified and it is morally wrong. Shame on you for stealing from the homeless. Yes, that's right – it's theft; you must take a long, hard look at the problems in this country.

I hope you read this book and understand what I'm trying to achieve. I will keep going until I see that I'm helping. Passing on knowledge is key to Scotland's recovery. We have people unemployed or homeless who would make excellent counsellors. We need to focus on the knowledge these people have. It won't happen overnight but it's a step in the right direction. Baby steps will soon turn into giant strides, then the country will see that it's working. There will always be folk trying to stop me or slow me down, but my mindset is that it's happening with or without these people. Hopefully when you see me trying, you'll want to help as I can't do it all on my own. I need a lot of help and I'm not afraid to ask.

Hopefully, you will see in the coming months and years that you can achieve your own goals. You may not even know what your calling is yet. I didn't at first, but when it hits your mind you will know. Don't think about what people will say or think of your newfound dreams.

This is the critical time for you to realise who is in control. If things are getting difficult then you must talk to yourself otherwise you won't be in control. I turned counting sheep into refusing heroin. My mind is so tuned in now that it's always conscious every day of negative comments. Loved ones, friends and strangers all have their own thoughts, but don't quite understand what is going on. If you are that happy in your own life that this makes no sense, then I'd urge you to share your happiness and positivity. It's people like me who needed to hear your thoughts about happiness.

Even if happiness is a long way away for you, you can still make positive changes – either baby steps or instantly changing, it doesn't matter. Two steps forward, one step back means you're still heading in the right direction. The one step back you block from your mind, relapse or whatever it is – just block it! Think about the good things you've done in your life and use those to keep you driving on.

Chapter 1

Everyone knows that drugs are bad, so why do so many people end up addicts? I was brought up in a loving family so I shouldn't have fallen into any traps. Yet my very first memory of heroin was growing up as a boy in Edinburgh.

We lived in Craigentinny, in the east of the city not far from the seaside resort of Portobello. From the early 80s until the late 90s we lived at Loganlea Terrace, then we moved to Loaning Road nearby. It was a much bigger flat and we four boys would still be room sharing, but if my big bro Kevin got his own room I'd get peace from him.

I was born on 2nd June in 1979. I'm told I was a cute baby. I found being the second eldest of four boys really difficult. Kevin was three years older than me, Mark three years younger. Kyle came along four years after Mark.

My dad was strict and amazing at sports so we were always competing for his attention. Believe me, I tried my heart out but it was clear I wasn't going to be competing for any attention at all. Football was our drug of choice as a family – we are all daft Hibees fans. However, Kevin had a Hearts scarf around one of his teddies (sorry, bro!) when he was a wee boy, before seeing sense and jumping ship later. It was clear my two younger brothers were going to be gifted footballers, so I really didn't stand a chance. I was never first at anything. Mark, three years younger, was just as fast as me and then came his chance to go to Ian St John's football camp. I of course was overlooked for this massive opportunity. I instead got dragged all over the country to *watch*.

Most of my memories are of jealousy, and maybe that's why my choices define me. I was always a troubled soul and felt like I was adopted. They used to taunt me, all of them – Mum and Dad included – that I'd been found in a dustbin.

I would act up for my mum and dad purposely just so they would shout at me. Occasionally arses got skelped in my house and my dad would line us four boys up with a belt in hand. I was never in front and Kevin was always at the back, Mark would get belted and scream the house down so much so it made my dad feel sorry for us. I don't mind admitting I was crying my eyes out and so were the other two. It wasn't child abuse, it was just to give us a scare and teach us not to be bad. But it turned out being bad was going to be my choice to get attention regardless of the red arses it would get me.

I was automatically integrated into a gang from as early back as I can remember. A group of friends is a group of friends until you start committing crimes. We were a bad lot, to be honest, but we showed amazing loyalty to each other when outside forces came to Craigentinny and started to cause trouble. We showed very little respect to our elders and they didn't seem to be able to stop us. We would smash everything in our path, so the police would come give us a chase. There were too many chases to mention them all, but I'll tell you a few of the most memorable.

We used to go to the posh houses on Britwell Crescent, then head all the way to the Land Rover garage, to do the back greens of the wealthy. Big walls and prickly hedges alike; too many dogs, though. These gardens all had apple trees that produced little red cooking apples which made amazing missiles. I'm ashamed to think of the damage to property I caused, but if you didn't you couldn't be in the YCT (Young Craigentinny Toonland gang).

I remember smashing the window of a big bungalow and waiting for the man to come out. The longer you waited, the more courage you had. All I did though was look around and see who I was faster than. On this particular night I was with two friends I knew I could beat in a race so I was confident I wouldn't get caught. A light went on, then the porch light then there was the click of the door. I took one look at the boy and shouted 'OH FUCK!'

We bolted straight away as this guy appeared not happy at all and more than willing to chase us. I'll never forget his breath as he was catching me up, but he ignored me and ran straight after the fastest runners who were overconfident. He caught one of my friends, no problem. The man gripped him by the collar and marched him back to his house. But we soon turned on the man and threw our apples at him until he let our pal go.

The primary school and park were our territory and many an adult got leathered up and down for just walking past. We were just young teenagers, but we also had the guys like Brad and Willie who were grown men in their mid 20s. We were an intimidating bunch as often as twenty or thirty of us would gather regularly.

Drugs were on the scene as soon as the boys started going to Leith Academy. At nights they would appear with joints of hash. Kevin hated me hanging about because I would grass on him if he smoked it. I took many a belt from Kevin, but nothing like the time Brad

4

dropped the joint at his feet – Kevin was miles away and would never see me, I thought. As soon as I puffed it, Brad warned me of Kevin's imminent arrival. Thirty or so of us were out that night but he didn't hold back. He grabbed my jacket and threw me up off my feet against the school wall, then belted me over the head (no Mark to grass him to Mum).

That seemed to be the way my and Kevin's relationship went, at least until my 21st party at the postie club. I confessed to him and Stuart, my cousin, on the bench outside that heroin had gotten me and from that day everything changed. He has been nothing but supportive ever since.

The first time I got into trouble with the police, I must have been nine or ten years old. We were in the arcades in Portobello and we decided to go into the toilets that were just beside. There was a box of matches that had spilled on the floor. I was a bit of a firebug back then so I picked up a match, went into the toilet and lit the match against the grout between the tiles at the mirror. The match lit and it was going to burn my finger, so I dropped it in the bin, which was filled with paper towels. The bin began to go on fire.

Unbeknown to me a security guard was sitting in a cabin inside the public toilets. He came out straightaway, grabbed me by the scruff of my neck and marched me to Portobello police station, where I had to sit and wait on my dad because my mum was working. So, I'd been a little bit of an arsonist; it wasn't on purpose but that was my first involvement with the police.

For most of my life I have stayed out of trouble with the law, although I have committed crimes that I am not proud of. The more serious crimes that I probably could have ended up committing, I didn't. I am proud of myself for some of the things, especially when I was on heroin and things were really hard, that I didn't do. Some of the things that other people did do – robbing and stealing – that was never me. I was a beggar and borrower, and I would scrounge from folk to get my drugs.

The next times I got in trouble were all car offences.

Approaching going to secondary I was really nervous and ugly – buck teeth, a ton of plukes and horrible, thick hair. Everyone would take the piss and Kevin didn't like me, I thought. This was going to be difficult. In my first week at Leith Academy I managed to get lost going to the toilet. I couldn't find it as the place was massive and full of corridors. I remember getting a horrible pain in the base of my spine just before I full-blown pissed myself. Luckily, the science teacher passed first and not my mates. He sent me home before lunch so I thought everyone would find out. The following day nobody said anything, so I just carried on as usual.

Most of my secondary days were spent trying to get noticed. Girls started showing up at nights from Leith and I knew nobody I fancied would ever look at me. My only chance was to be funny and make a fool of myself. I got loads of warm smiles, hugs and pecks on the cheek, but never a bag-off. In fact, I went into my working life at 16 before I ever even tried to snog a girl. With my teeth and big lips, it got messy.

I got a job straight from school at Crawfords the bakers and I absolutely loved it. Mr Blobby cakes galore. I soon realised I was on my own as bullies started on me at work. I had friends too, but not the YCT.

Adulthood wasn't easy but I was earning my own dollar. As soon as 17 hit, I got my licence to drive a car, a little blue Fiesta. I finally found freedom to explore on my own. I loved driving up town, tunes blaring with the windows down, a fag in the mouth, FWD burnouts everywhere. That's until I was going up the cobbles of West Bow Street or the Grassmarket. I managed to slide into a very high kerb and wrote my first car off. I had to sit for two hours waiting on my mum, with the recovery driver showing up at 3am. Just as the clubs were coming out, too, drunk people laughing and trying to rock the car back and forth.

For my next car, I went to my cousin Danny's garage. I had a look about but my car was chosen for me, a brown Nissan Cherry 1.3s (s for sport). It was horrible but it was that or nothing, so I took it. Five doors, very nippy and comfortable, but it was still a brown Cherry.

It did the trick, but next time at the garage I saw this mouldy, run-down Escort XR3 sitting in the corner. 'It's broken,' Danny told me, so I went home after he fixed the Nissan Cherry.

The following week I was back and the Escort was away. I arranged to go on a road trip to Ireland with Bill, Darren and Willie. Just as I was telling my mum, 'I am going and it's up to me, I'm an adult now', she said to me: 'You go to Ireland but you won't get what your dad's got for you.'

We were getting supplies from Scotmid when I saw my dad driving a black, minted XR3! It was gleaming, with all panels replaced. He passed by waving, so I ran as fast as I could all the way home. Ireland was on hold. I'll never forget driving along Princes Street on a sunny afternoon with the sun roof open. The boy racer was here at last, REC 270Y.

I loved that car.

With a lovely car like that the girls would surely notice me. Perhaps I would finally get to kiss a girl properly – a bag-off, a smooch or, as we called it, tongues! Eighteen and I had never kissed a girl properly; a few failed attempts but nothing ever worked out. I was all teeth and banged the teeth of the girl's mouth or cut their lips. I got so nervous I often froze.

The car really did get me attention from girls. Drinking and driving don't mix so I'd have to pick, get pissed and try pull a bird, or drive around nightclubs at night hoping girls would have beer goggles on and find me attractive. I was ugly my whole life and no amount of spot cream, gel or hair mousse would change that.

I finally bagged off in the back seat after picking three girls up with Darren. He pulled one girl but the one I fancied looked at me and said: 'Come on then, FFS.' I chucked everyone out the car, drove round the corner and springboked into the back seat. If she'd never just jumped on me I would have bottled it, for sure. Bag-off done, out the way. I was now no longer focused on sex; that could wait for now because another love was destined for me.

Chapter 2

I started going to my cousin's pub for a pint for the first time legally. I drank alcohol `since I was 15, but nothing good ever came out of drinking when I was young. I was always the butt of the jokes, often self-inflicted just for the attention.

When I was 18 the only illegal drug I had taken was cannabis and even then I didn't fancy the feeling that I got but because all my friends were smoking it I used to join in. It was always the same for years, we would all chip in and get a bit of smoke. Weekends would usually involve alcohol along the way. You could get grass, hash, soap bar, soft black or trips with ease back then. Then things started to change; suddenly we found ourselves wrapped in tinfoil and milky bar wrappers.

My friends always came in for me every day because of the car, but on this particular day nobody arrived. As the hours passed I gave up waiting and went for a drive down Portobello beach. As I pulled up I saw my friend's tiny wee Fiesta crammed full of my friends. So I pulled alongside, but they totally ignored me. I had not fallen out with anybody, so what was going on?

Eventually Steve opened the window a tiny bit and said, 'Can I come to you?' As he opened the door, I saw my first flash of tin foil, followed by a bellow of smoke. Daryl started shouting, 'Shut the fucking door!' I asked Steve what was going on and he said, chasing the dragon.

'WTF is that?' I asked 'What kind of dragon?'

'Heroin,' he replied.

I had always been anti drugs and I soon realised that's why I wasn't involved. I didn't like it so I offered a couple of them to jump in my car. I was curious and you know what happened to the cat. In my case the dragon ate it.

I had let them smoke dope in my car so I knew by their eyes. They were red and glazed and they told me they were smoking heroin. Shocked was an understatement. It didn't make sense to take heroin. Everybody knew it kills you eventually. I was so naïve at that moment. We were all taught that at school and parents were very strict when it came to breaking the law. That was always our belief growing up in the 80s, 90s and 00s.

I will always remember watching Steve and Daryl in my back seat, chasing this brown blob with a silver tube down a piece of tin foil. It was an art to have the lighter in the right place, my friends told me. They went on and on about how good it was, although they didn't look too happy to me.

I was the last of a group of nine or ten of us who would try it. Robert, Bob, Adam and Brad were all glue sniffers, and gas too. Brain thought he was Bruce Lee. They all did, actually, but Bob climbed the primary school roof and did it for all to see. There were no heroin dealers in our area so I used to take them to Niddrie and Bingham to get it, but I wasn't trying it. I'd sit in my car while the ringleader ran into the stairwell, returning ten nerve-racking minutes later with a big grin on his face. We would then head to the beach as normal.

I never went near it for two weeks. Then one day, while sitting at the beach, I tried it in anger for having a bad day as I'd had an argument at home. I could remember buzzing a tin of gas when I was 11 but I never inhaled, just pushed it against my tooth. Anyway, all I had to do was inhale. 'Don't touch the tooter or the blob of brown,' Bob explained.

So I took a hit and it was disgusting, tasted of fish and stank like it, too. I went white as a sheet, maybe even green. I got out of the car and coughed so bad. I felt sick. I sweated badly and felt dizzy and was just gone in a world with just me in it and nobody else would matter. My life with heroin was about to start.

Me being me, I tried it again and again. To this day I'll never know why I ever went back. It was the same as when I took the fag ends out the ashtray and smoked them. I started smoking cigarettes at 15 and it was very similar, only this time I felt far away, spinning and spinning in my head… a bumblebee flew in and I just lay watching it for ten minutes.

I continued to go back for more until one day a few weeks later Reece said to me: 'Do you know you're addicted now?' I laughed and said: 'Shut up.'

I never did try to stop at that point, or even find out. The drug had taken me to a place where I didn't care so much about anything anymore. Months passed. It was clear it was affecting us all. Money was the first issue. If you had it you were ok and everyone bum-sucked you. If you didn't, then you were in trouble.

You can't just rock up at a dealer's door and ask for a bag (smack). 'People will stab you,' Daryl explained, so only he could go to the door. We all chipped in a few quid each to get £20 quid together. We were always sad en route to Niddrie because the sweats were here. Everyone looked sore, like wincing a lot and I didn't feel great. Maybe this was my two weeks' grace because they looked ill.

Right enough, a few weeks later I started to withdraw like nothing mattered. I needed a hit. Stomach cramps, eyes watering, sniffles and the pain in my stomach was unbearable, like decked over in pain almost.

When we finally got a bag, OMG it was party in the car time. Tunes blaring, everybody crashing, cigs, everybody high and bouncing my car from one side to the other. The suspension always took a hit on our way home. It didn't matter, we had smack and would have warmth soon. Everybody worked together like soldiers to prepare the tooter, foil and lighters with plenty of gas. Zippos or anything with a big flame was a no-no, you could lose your smack by burning it.

Once we started, whoever had it got to go first. Daryl of course. Anyway, it would soon come to me. Daryl always controlled the lighter so you just tooted behind this blob of brown and inhaled all the smoke you can. It always caught your throat and was wasted. I always thought you could have a wider tooter, but you never really had time as it is without trying some origami shit building one. A tooter's just a silver tube roughly the size of a cigarette. The warmth is followed by an itchy nose and heavy eyelids. I won't lie, it felt amazing!

Gouching was normal in our group, I think that's why it didn't bother me in the army. We leaned up against each other all the time, slavering, jaws dropping, druggies the lot of us. A bunch of lovely men had been taken by the drug that is heroin. Everyone does things that they are ashamed of and I have done loads in life, as you're about to read.

We often smoked it in the car so Dumbass here was on heroin, driving. I feel so guilty for the things I did while on drugs. Being reckless and uncaring is lethal. Luckily, I got my car taken off me, but not before I had an accident.

The accident was at the King's Road roundabout in Portobello. This is where I lost my driver's licence. Well, I didn't actually lose it there and then, but that was the start of the circumstances that took my licence away. I came to an opening at the roundabout. It was raining and a cyclist was coming round. He had indicated he was coming off and down into Portobello High Street, and as I was coming out of Portobello High Street he slipped and slid into my front wheel. He was ok. I think he hurt himself a little on the chin but there were no broken bones.

It was my fault as I shouldn't even have been on the road. I had seen him but to this day I would say he did indicate he was coming off there. I had taken speed that day and knew I would get lifted. I took off and went home.

I got pulled over the next time I was in the car, the following week. A police officer wearing a hi-vis jacket ran out into the middle of the road, put his arm up and shouted 'Stop'.

'Aye, it was me who was driving,' I said.

He took his notepad out and, shit, I was bust. Devastated is an understatement. I couldn't afford the car anyway. Insurance was a big thing in our family, none of us were allowed cars without insurance. I was on foot now with no or very little money, but I still had my job at Safeway.

The next brush with the law was when I was waiting for all this court stuff to come through. I'd had to get rid of my XR3 because of the insurance and the cost of fuel. I ended up getting a smaller-engined Astra 1.2. A few weeks later I was with all the boys and we went to the Asda car park at The Jewel in Edinburgh to smoke heroin in the car. One of the trolley boys spotted us and called the police, unbeknown to me. I was sitting with the key in the ignition so we could have the heater on when two police cars arrived. I was arrested and taken to Leith police station.

I deserved that. It wasn't something that had even crossed my mind, but reflecting back it was just the wrong thing to do, so the police arriving and arresting me was well deserved. At that point I only wanted my heroin. I wasn't really interested in losing my licence, being fined, or what my mum and dad or my family would say. I had heroin on me at the time of the arrest so my sole focus was getting home so that I could smoke it. At the police station I admitted to smoking cannabis, so I lost my licence from that point.

However, the following week I decided to drive the car not anywhere in Edinburgh, but to Longniddrie Bents. We pulled up thinking we were being smart going away miles away. We had literally only just pulled up. A police car had followed me all the way through Musselburgh, saying we had looked suspicious. That was a week after I had been arrested. The police officers were really nice that day, they could have been a lot harsher. We had a bit of hash so decided to give them that instead of the heroin. I think they could see we were in trouble with drugs and stuff. But we got a stern warning and were told to return home.

So I lost my licence for a few years. I had a drug problem, so I wasn't going to be on the road driving, I was going to be getting the bus and walking everywhere. That was the start of another chapter where I was going to have to do everything on foot. There was a lot of danger involved in drug use and the sourcing of it, and there was a lot of robbing and stabbings, and getting bumped. It made it so much more difficult if you didn't have a car to jump into.

I started spending less time with my YCT friends and more time with my Safeway friends, Sam and Harry. They really took me under their wing and tried to show me a different life. Of course, I wasn't ready and continued to smoke heroin on my lunch breaks and in toilets or in mates' cars. I never thought I would be able to kick the habit. It was just a part of my life and I was never going to attract any girls, especially not now. My weight was dropping fast and my eyes were always pinned.

All those dark days I had laughs, too, especially in Safeway. I started in hygiene with Veronica and Sheila. I'm sure my dad pulled some strings with Carl to get me the job. I left school at 16 but my first proper job was doing dishes every Friday and Saturday night at The Jolly. Victor was the owner and he really looked after me: £10 for the Friday shift and £15 for the Saturday. At 15 years old, £25 was a lot to me. It all ended up in the bookies anyways, but that's for a different time.

I really enjoyed my job, especially in the produce department. Fruit was better than pish and sick, like in hygiene. Euan was my boss. To this day I'll always appreciate how he helped me out. Timothy hated me and we often fought; Timothy was Euan's right-hand man. We had a team of four or five guys working the shifts during the day and it was physically challenging – sacks of potatoes were our barbells at work. I sweated a lot and that wasn't helped by going cold turkey at work. Heroin was difficult to get and I needed an alternative.

I decided to buy methadone to ease the pain a bit. Holy shit, it worked! I drank 10mls of green syrup and two minutes later, the warmth – OMG... It was cheaper and you got it prescribed. If you measure it methadone is stronger and the hit lasts longer. I took myself to the doctors to get a prescription for two or three weeks. It worked but heroin was everywhere. I ended up taking both once to properly do some damage. I can't write about that time as it is a complete blur.

Talking of blurs, Valium is the worst. All the years I was on Valium there are few stories about it as I can't remember. A brilliant drug and I use them to this day to fly, so I don't have a bad word to say about them. A lie, sorry. I do actually. These vallies make you Superman, as in you feel invincible; I would go places I otherwise would be too scared to. Heroin comes first, though, and no amount of vallies will ever take my pain away. I've lost patches of my life because of my addiction to Valium. I was on every opiate I could get and hash – when you mixed these you got really stoned. Add Valium into the mix and you really do have a lethal cocktail.

I was physically and mentally drained and this job wasn't going to last. We had a ton of laughs, though. Sam, Harry, Mike, Jimmy and Jamie always picked me up. I know I was hard work because selfishness and heroin go hand in hand; you're fully aware of what you're doing, but the thought of cold turkey was enough to drive me to beg for money from the people I loved most.

I never took to stealing like my friends did. My face always told the story, so when my friends would go to the supermarkets I always gave them away by the shock that they were filling their pants and jackets with bacon, steak, fish... basically anything you could sell. We knew who would buy it straightaway, so it fed the habit. I never had a problem with them stealing from supermarkets. Stealing from people is shocking at any time, but thankfully most of our group actually had jobs and loving families behind them so they always got bailed out.

All I had to do was hide it until I could stop. That was always after you'd had a hit, famous last words. I managed quite well hiding it until I was 21. That night on my 21st I admitted heroin had taken me. I smoked my big bag of smack while listening to my new Stereophonics CD. The love I felt that night was unbelievable. Overwhelming, it turned out. Heroin and alcohol don't mix well.

Chapter 3

My family were what held me together. I'd seen early in life how hard my parents worked to keep us in clothes: four boys who had a knack of destroying trainers through playing football, clothes too, and often hand-me-downs. In fact I got clothes from both directions, Mark took over in size in primary school so I got Kevin's hand-me-downs and Mark got hand-me-ups. It really was a strain for my mum and dad bringing us up. We were all little shits who fought constantly until in our twenties. It wasn't only the clothes that came both ways, there was the kicking and biting from Mark, when he was five or so, and the punching. Wrestlemania every day because there were only two biscuits left and there were four of us. Split them, I hear you say. Well, that never happened. Not with my brothers, the greedy wee shits! We always had each other's back though. Even Kevin stuck up for me loads. I know he loved me and those times confirmed that.

I was annoying growing up, always joking around, never listening. I later realised that I began talking to myself from early on. If I thought I didn't fit in I could always put headphones on and listen to my music. Most of my life I have only heard music, never listened. Then when depression took over, I found myself immersed so far into songs that I felt the emotions physically: happy, sad, angry, a few others. I was purposely looking for music that sounded sad. I didn't deserve to be happy for putting my family through the hell that was heroin.

I had worked myself into a downward spiral that I couldn't even slow down. Antidepressants didn't help, they just made me a zombie. Nothing there, no emotions at all. I later realised it was only prolonging the problem. I didn't want to be alive anymore. This world was horrible, full of hate and anger. I saw so many horrible things. Some I took really hard. I saw so much cruelty that I knew I would never be evil like that. My problem was going to be staying alive, as these thoughts were getting more frequent. I finally decided I would take a ton of pills. Hopefully I would sleep and be at peace, no more helplessness. I only ever wanted to see people laughing and smiling. I will always feel guilty for doing that to them and I can't ever change that. To repair some of the damage was going to be a big ask.

I relapsed so many times and music defined me. I became what I heard, but listening to actual lyrics was saving my life. I would pick sad-sounding songs because that's what I thought I deserved. On reflection, the positive messages in these songs were keeping me going. I will say to anyone suffering from addictions that you can use music to influence your own life. It will only work if you believe it can be done, so you really need to focus on your mind. The little voice can start talking positively and start to run the show. Do you want to be happy? If the answer is yes, then please take on board what I'm trying to say. You control your own choices. It's not easy to change your mind from negative to positive, or is it?

If you were asked to start hating someone or something and go from positive to negative then you could do that easier. It's exactly the same: trust you have a good heart and make the changes needed for a better, happier you. Unhappy humans will try to sway you from your goals, but this is just a test. Loved ones and friends will all have negative comments at some time during your recovery, but you don't focus on them. Stay positive or it won't work!

The messages in music saved my life. Everybody Hurts by R.E.M. was the actual song. Michael Stipe touched my heart that night, singing for me to hold on and I reacted by not taking my own life. I used to cut my arms up because I wanted people to know I was in trouble. How do you confess to feeling suicidal? Songs are positive messages. It's amazing that I've managed to work out what went on in my own life, especially with the suicidal thoughts. I'm not even annoyed that it's taken me until I'm 40.

I can't blame anyone else for the bad choices I've made. I can only learn from my mistakes. I recently realised that I was preparing to die for such a long time. I never thought I'd reach 40, or 30 for that matter. Since I've moved outside Edinburgh, things have become so clear in my head. I fully understand what was happening all these years ago, even in recent times when I've been struggling. I don't know what was causing it. Your mind controls your body. No, your mind controls everything. When you start understanding how to have an actual grip on your mind so that you can change information that is stored then you can change your life. It all begins with talking to yourself – we all do it, that person inside your head making decisions can be vanquished!

Create a positive voice/person in your mind. Only when you accept that this is possible, can you implement the changes you need. The way I explain it is the information you see/hear is stored in your mind; your mind isn't something you mess about with, but if sadness has taken your heart then your mind can help combat that. For someone like me who was always sad and angry, it's difficult to take when you fix your own mind. Why didn't I know before now that you can deflect all the negative things?

I have lived a whole different life inside my own head, telling myself that I was going to die soon. In the forefront of my mind were lectures from my parents and teachers and I purposely blocked everything from doctors and counsellors. I think I chose the negative, self-destructive route because of guilt. I was so ashamed in my heart that I could fill myself with self-pity.

Chapter 4

Heroin wasn't my only drug of choice, I've taken crack, magic mushrooms, LSD, cocaine, MSTs and all the prescribed medications going, ecstasy, amphetamines, all ranges of cannabis. I'll be missing some and I'm in no way proud of it. I can't change my past but I can use my knowledge to help.

Crack was only an option because the heroin had dried up. We were all ill and sitting on my mate's bed, all eyes on this tiny wee rock that looked like smack but cost a lot more. We set up the pipe and I was the fourth hit. The first three just inhaled it as you would heroin, so I breathed that smoke way down into my lungs, held it in for as long as I could and waited on a chaser. A chaser was something we often did with joints of cannabis, even tobacco. You just inhale both at once. This crack wasn't going to make us feel better but I'd have taken any drugs at that point.

I remember feeling amazing for a short time. I'm not here to lie – I can see why so many struggle with this drug. It didn't last long and before we knew it discussions had started about spending what little money we had left on another bit of crack. Funny how nobody had any money before we smoked it; as soon as everyone had taken a hit the pockets were emptied. Everyone loving life, smiles and laughs everywhere. An hour later it was wearing off and our addiction to heroin was showing itself once again.

Magic mushrooms was my most memorable drug, I've taken them once and I'll never, ever take them again. Wow, just wow! We sneaked up to my house and made cups of tea, boiled the mushrooms then added them to our cups. We all took a fair amount and I was not prepared for the things I was about to see. Not hallucinations, this shit was for real.

I remember everything vividly. The first thing we did was jump back in the car. We waited ten minutes, then started laughing so hard that we couldn't breathe properly, bright red faces. We went to a friend's house – he was the leader of our gang and his girlfriend didn't touch drugs, so when we rocked up we tried to behave. My other friend was so quiet and shy usually, but even he was acting strange.

We were watching a documentary about wildlife when out of nowhere my quiet friend picked up a chisel and launched it straight at the window. He hit the wooden frame. That was it, we were chucked out straightaway. We walked round to the chippy and went inside. My quiet friend reached over, picked up a brown sauce bottle and squirted it all over the man serving. The man jumped up on the counter but my other friend calmed him down before any trouble broke out.

Mushrooms had turned my quiet friend into a lunatic. He started grabbing people's hair as they passed by and then stand like a statue; as soon as they walked on he would run up and do it again. I headed back to the chippy for my hamburger chip roll and didn't see him again until later that night. We were passing by in the car and saw a jumper in the middle of the road. It was my mate's. A further two hundred yards down the road were his jeans, again in the middle of the road. They had the belt and boxers inside too. I picked up all his clothes and we took them to the police station. The officer at the desk told us a report had just come in that a naked man covered in mud had walked into a pub not too far away and lain down. It was him for sure so we headed to his house and sneaked round the back to his bedroom. He had walked into the living room holding a lightbulb, we later found out.

Magic mushrooms lasted that one night, thankfully. Those kinds of drugs will affect your mind more than any other in the long term. I've seen many people lose that fight and it's not nice. LSD was the same, so I only ever took a few trips and never really enjoyed them. I was a stoner and needed opiates. Occasionally I would take cocaine, but only ever if gifted. I've never bought it in my life because I've seen first-hand the dangers of it. If I'm getting high then I've already sourced my opiates and I'd rather spend my money on an ecstasy tablet or some bass. Bass is just pure amphetamine – I loved it. It gave me the confidence to talk to girls but that's all you could do as my manhood would shrivel up to nothing. At the time I didn't care. I would dance and girls would join in so I was happy. Knowing my heroin was at home made me relaxed. I had lots of amazing nights out with friends, but I'd pick heroin over a girl every time. Heroin overcame all horrible feelings – drunk, hungover, on a comedown, it didn't matter. My heroin would fix it. I cared what people thought of me and drugs helped to make me not care.

Let me explain my knowledge of MSTs. They are blue pills with a time-release coating. We would scrape that off and break them in two because they were so strong and lasted ages, even longer than methadone. They gave you a strong, heavy stone and at times I preferred them to heroin.

Most folk know about cannabis. I will say this: every drug will have negative effects somewhere. However, I will defend cannabis and go as far as to say it should be legalised. I understand people are against drugs, but this one is better than alcohol and that's legal. The medicinal applications this drug has are amazing. People all over the globe report how good it is for various diseases.

Cannabis comes in many varieties: soft black, slate, soap bar, pollen, weed or grass, and tons more. I always preferred solid as the weed was too strong for me. I sold solid for a few years to help keep me alive and generally that's all I smoked. I can remember some moments in life when I had weed and made some pretty big decisions. Weight training, I was smoking weed. Boxing training, I was smoking weed. I'm unsure about when I stopped taking heroin, but it's possible I was smoking weed. It honestly broadens your mind and inspires me. Its pros easily outweigh the cons, in my opinion.

Chapter 5

I carried on searching for jobs for months, but I gave up. Nobody was going to employ someone who asked to borrow money at an interview: 'Can you give me an advance on a job you're not going to give me?' I could still drive, so I decided to risk taking a delivery job. I had nothing and needed heroin so badly, even methadone or MST – just something to stop the pain.

Selling drugs was my only option, I would buy half a nine bar of cannabis already chopped up into half-ounces in a money bag. If I could sell it all in a week, I could fund my habit and always have a bit of cannabis to smoke too. I had a ton of friends who smoked it so I undercut everyone by a fiver so I could get customers. They all visited me anyway so it didn't feel that wrong. Of course, I know now it's wrong. It should be legalised. Back then, though, hash was nothing respected folk in the community would smoke. Heroin was the problem, or opiates to be fair.

You learn to run a business. I'd barely started selling hash when I got the opportunity to get thousands of blues. These drugs were amazing for knocking you out and you were also invincible and invisible! It wasn't long before the druggies started swarming and my door was always open to everyone. Chucky (borrowing) was my downfall. I would let folk off all the time. I was making money from the hash and vallies so I didn't mind, they would keep me company in the dark times.

People start taking drugs for lots of different reasons, but the kind of drug usually changes at some point along the line. It wasn't until I started talking to drug users properly about their addictions that I started to understand why people use different kinds of drugs. All drugs have different effects and all have negative side effects.

I used drugs to escape my reality and I was greedy, often using when there was no need. I would take more drugs out of boredom. If you don't have a hobby there is a good chance you'll be doing the same thing. Hobbies or other interests are really important to recovery, it doesn't matter what they are, what matters is you put something else in your mind to focus on.

For me it was weights. I had a set of dumbbells in my flat and one night when I was watching Rocky films, I felt the need to start doing push-ups. I was smoking grass at the time! Then I picked up the dumbbells and started to do curls. It felt so good. With music blasting away, my motivation increased day by day. I noticed muscles I never knew existed. I was less angry and dreamed of what it would be like to go to a gym and train properly. I trained in the flat for a few months until I felt comfortable nobody would laugh. I didn't know back then what I know now, so I wasn't aware exactly what I was doing.

I was switching my hobby from taking extra drugs to exercising. I still used certain drugs, but could see a better me at last. Physically too – my appetite improved and I started eating protein and loads of fibre. That was my turning point. Mentally I was still struggling, but I had more hope now than I ever had in the past.

Heroin may not kill me after all, I would often fantasise. As time passed, I grew in strength and not only physically. Mentally I was already blocking some negative suicidal thoughts.

Chapter 6

I often get asked what it's like to take heroin and, to be honest, it's amazing. That's not to say I think you should try it. The opposite, in fact. The reason there are so many people addicted to heroin is that it blocks your reality. A massive cloud comes over all your emotions. If you're depressed, like I was, then it maybe seems like an option. Trust me, it's not. Yes, depression leaves you for the short term, but the health risks are outrageous.

At first you take it and enter an almost coma-like state; you're conscious of everything that's going on around you, but you just can't move. You enter into a very heavy daydream where life is bliss and you have no worries. That might seem great but the problems start when it starts to wear off. You slowly come back to reality and all you can think about is your next hit. You want to re-enter that cloud.

The problem is heroin is highly addictive. Although at the beginning you feel like you're in control, you actually are far from it. You've started taking it for a reason and heroin isn't a cure. All you're doing is prolonging the agony and adding a whole new chapter to it. You tell yourself you can stop anytime you want, which makes it easier to take it. Then after a few weeks, when your money is low or you can't get any, you decide it's okay because you can't be addicted. Wrong! It grabbed you and you never knew it.

The physical side of withdrawal is at first just like having the flu. You think: 'I'm totally addicted and it ain't so bad so I'll just get one more fix and then stop the next time.' A few weeks later you run out of cash again and decide this time you will definitely stop, only this time the flu is more severe. It's then you start to worry and stress about what's going on. At this point there's only one way to stop the anxiety. Heroin is the cure you know, so again you get your last fix and this time you will stop after it. Yeah, of course you won't.

You're fully aware that you are getting deeper in, but it's just easier to forget and get wasted. Heroin will fully absorb you and you will think about little else. When you're taking it, you're already thinking about your next hit. Things are great when you have an endless pot of gold and a dealer with an endless supply. The shit hits the fan when either of them finish. You need more money, so you borrow and have every intention of paying it back so it doesn't seem a problem at the time.

When your dealer dries up and you need to seek out a new dealer, that's when it becomes very dangerous. Unless you're known, many dealers won't entertain you, but you're a source of income for many who can't pick and choose who they sell too. Buying drugs on the street is the worst thing ever. You're both strangers who want something each other has. The difference is you can inspect a £20 note with a glance and touch; you can't do the same with a tiny bit of powder – brick dust and women's face powder are two things I've purchased on the streets.

Trust me, when you've spent a whole day gathering money and now your withdrawals are really bad you don't care what you buy. You just hope the people don't bump you. Thankfully, it was just rubbish deals we had to cope with mostly.

There were always too many heads round the tooter and soon we started to split up as a group. All the sneakiness started and we were all struggling with our addictions.

Chapter 7

I have a big family and a ton of amazing friends. The support I've received over the years has kept me going in times of darkness. My wife, obviously, plays a major role in my sanity now, but back then it was my parents and brothers. I deserved to be ignored for what I had done to them. They all had their moments of frustration with me, but they never abandoned me.

My Auntie Dot played the biggest part in keeping me going. I visited often and she was so easy to talk with. I could speak to my Auntie Dot about anything. Sadly she is no longer with us, but she still lives in my heart and mind.

My brothers were all hard work growing up, but once I ended up on drugs I felt their pity and could see it in everyone's eyes. They no longer taunted me and I didn't like it. I'd rather they shouted and were angry. I didn't even deserve the pity. I was wallowing in it myself and I was drowning from thoughts of suicide or opiate use.

My friends helped me to escape my reality. Playing snooker, pool, golf, football and Xbox or Playstation was always a good distraction.

I love all my work friends from over the years, but none like when I joined the army. These friends will always be special to me as we all experienced the hell that is basic training together. I have close civilian friends, too, and they are special to me in their own way – always there to talk, but more importantly listen.

I've been lucky with close friends and family, so they have all played their part in my recovery. Although I feel happy and motivated now, there is always a chance I could slide downwards again. That's life and I'm not naïve enough to think it couldn't happen. I know one thing and that is I'll never take heroin again. My back is getting bad and my medication is at a pivotal point. I've reduced my medication, but I worry about the physical pain I'm in. I plan to try some different techniques, but surgery is the only way. I am still on my feet and relatively able so will soldier on for now. Maybe a new drug is out there, one with side effects I can handle. I can handle opiates now, but I'm tired of them. Co-codamol has served its purpose for my medical reasons, but my abuse of the tablets earlier in life means it feels wrong to be stuck on it.

Cannabis eases my pain, but I've no idea if it's enough on its own. I must try to find out, so I plan to detox once things are moving with the charity. I'm not beating myself up over this, though. I am feeling better already, so even on four tablets of co-codamol a day it's better for me. Miracles can happen so maybe there is something that can be done.

Living with the physical pain has been a walk in the park compared to what going back onto opiates has been. I can see a possible way out but only time will tell. Abusing these drugs is so much easier because they are widely used and prescribed by doctors. If I had an endless supply of heroin, I probably would have ended up overdosing.

Some of my family and friends get prescribed different medications so when I've been stuck in the past I have had a lifeline somewhere. I cried a few months back because the doctors messed up my paperwork when I moved over to Fife. They refused me my prescription and I ran out completely. I felt helpless and I panicked that I would be going cold turkey that night, not because I was wanting off them but because I couldn't get them. My mind played a horrible game that day and took me back to my days of sweats, shivers, fever, migraines and a horrible coldness. Climbing the walls, can't settle for anything, snapping at everyone. Numb-hearted and in need of drugs *again*.

This is something that I'm just learning to control. I need to share my thoughts in case they can help someone somewhere. Just one person and this guilt and shame is eased. I'll never rid myself of the guilt and shame as you can never turn back time... at least not yet. Or can you?

Chapter 8

I had been on heroin for five years when I decided enough was enough. I had said many times that I would get clean, but never actually believed that I could. I had gone cold turkey a couple of times, but that was mostly due to not being able to get any. This time was different. I had money and I could get it. I was going to be a dad and that was a good enough reason for me. I tried twice to go cold turkey and failed miserably after two days. I knew it wouldn't be easy but each time was unbearable and I was weak-minded.

I needed some help so I decided to go to the doctor. I remember saying about three words before breaking down in tears trying to explain my situation. After an hour or so of trying to explain it was decided that I should go to a drug clinic called Turning Point.

Turning Point dealt with drug users every day so I was hopeful that they could help me. I was very nervous and thought about turning back many times. I arrived and was offered tea or juice, then told to wait in the waiting room. It had massive sofas, the comfiest I have ever sat on. After about ten minutes a man called Keith came in and had to wake me up. I'd taken a little heroin that morning just to get me through the day and I crashed out not long after sitting down. I made my apologies after wiping the saliva from my mouth and he led me into his office.

Just like at the doctors, I got about three words in before breaking into tears. Again I had to explain my situation. Once I had finished, he asked me about my drug intake. I told Keith that I was a heroin addict but wanted to stop. He was a lovely man with a big heart, but looked to pass me over to his colleague Frank. Now Frank was an ex heroin addict and I remember switching on a bit when he told me; you never died, I remember thinking.

I still wasn't ready, but I had to show I was trying just to keep the peace. I did try but my mind wasn't in the right place. I didn't believe it was possible. I was still very negative in my thinking.

Chapter 9

I hadn't planned parenthood for obvious reasons, but the day I saw that wee button nose it melted my heart. I would be a good dad, but drugs would cause complications. Unfortunately, my only happy memories of when my daughter was wee was when it was just the two of us. I frequently fought with her mum, Ivy, and it was a horrible situation. I would stay in a different room, swallow my tablets then play on my console. The arguments were always both ways. I'm ashamed to say I hit her but it was never meant, we used to roll about on the floor as my heroin was number one always.

Then my daughter came along and I wanted to change. Methadone helped with money – I didn't have to walk around Edinburgh hoping to score. I took dihydrocodeine on top of the methadone, not because I needed it physically but because I was trapped. I knew us fighting was damaging my daughter and I couldn't cope. The stories Ivy told were downright lies. The police were called after a domestic while we were in temporary accommodation and even the officers called her out.

'He battered me. Arrest him!' she would scream.

The male officer took me in the room and asked what had happened. I told the truth.

'We have been out all day to get my fix and when we got home she picked my heroin up and hung it over the balcony. I grabbed her arm to get it back and then we ended up wrestling again. Josh was in the house at the time and he was rattling too. We just wanted left in peace to take it. I pointed in her face and accidentally poked her in the eye.'

The police officers both commented on her bruises, saying they were thumb marks most likely from restraint. Ivy ended up getting a telling off for saying I was battering her. I have never battered anyone in my life. I did defend myself which doesn't make it right. Guilt has followed me and will continue to do so. I'm guilty of a lot of things but not for hitting women, or hitting anyone actually.

I needed to stay away as much as possible for my daughter's sake. She was three when I left. It was my choice, though, and that had to be the case. The poor bairn was screaming with her hands over her ears as we wrestled, I'd had enough and wanted to leave but Ivy had locked the door. I was screaming for her to look at the bairn but she wouldn't.

One last time I grappled with her until I managed to force my way out the door. I ran, she followed – for about a mile anyway. I went through back greens and she couldn't keep up.

I hate writing this as it's horrible but that's what it was like – me focused on drugs and Ivy unhappy because I was ignoring her. I thought that was better than arguing, but she blew up anyway. One thing Ivy wasn't wrong about was that I was a druggie. And I would describe Ivy as a compulsive liar as I thought she had a hard time telling the truth.

We loved our bus journeys, me and the bairn. We would take her wee pink bag and fill it with Fruit Shoots, nappies and some chocolate. My friends had cars too and often picked us up. Our usual jaunts were to the beach or feeding ducks at Queen's Park. My daughter was spoiled by my family and friends.

I went for full custody a few weeks after I left, but because of my drug use it was unrealistic.

I had to say goodbye as it caused my first serious breakdown. The court had ordered me visitation rights, but Ivy wouldn't turn up. The final time I was supposed to get my daughter it was raining and I stood at the base of the statue for over an hour crying my eyes out. It destroyed me inside and if I wanted to live I must go better my own life. Not easy at all, but not impossible.

Maybe when she is older she will understand why I did what I did. I will never stop loving her, but chances are the poison will have set in.

Chapter 10

When I went to Turkey in 2001, it was with all my family – Auntie Dot, Uncle Duncan, Mum, Dad, Kevin, Mark, Kyle, Kevin's ex-wife Toni and their daughter Sally. It was my first ever holiday, my first time on a plane going abroad. And I was a heroin addict. I was also on methadone, so it was quite a big experience. I didn't have any money so my mum and dad agreed between them to pay for me, else I would have been the only one left behind.

When I got off the plane, I got culture shock for the first time in my life. It was unreal, heat, everywhere I looked it was crazy. I remember going to the supermarket and the hotel. We went down to the pool. Everybody was already in the pool, so I sat at the bar and ordered a beer. A young lad from Nottingham, Chris, came and sat beside me, asked me how I was doing.

I said: 'Sound, mate.'

We just hit it off. He was a DJ down on the beachfront, so he invited me to have a few beers in his room and listen to some music. Later that night we were going to go to the Banana Bar in Marmaris. And that's what we did.

Later that night, I made my excuses and disappeared away on my own. I went all the way down to the Banana Bar and, right enough, there was Chris DJing. When I walked in, he gave me a big shoutout and I remember feeling quite happy about that. I got free drinks for the rest of the night, half pints of vodka basically, if I remember right. They were just pouring straight from the bottle into my glass. I got absolutely hammered, but we had a brilliant night.

The following few days before Chris was to go home, we went out a few times and had an absolute blast. Chris's holiday ended, he went back to Nottingham and left me his card and stuff. One night I thought that it would be a good idea if I disappeared away on my own, so I went to the Banana Bar on my own. I had to pay for drinks this time. I sat there for ages, nobody really recognised me. So I just sat there and when the vodka took its toll and the dance music came on I was up on the bar dancing around. I wasn't the only one up on the bar. There were other folk but then they jumped down and I stayed up so I always remember jumping down off the bar, sitting down and then seeing half a dozen Turkish lads growling at me.

One of them put his two fingers together like a gun and put it to his head, indicating that, yeah, I might be getting shot here. I quickly skedaddled back to the apartment steaming drunk – I walked around for ages, couldn't find a taxi but eventually found a phone box and ended up phoning to find my way back.

The following morning didn't go down too well, because I'd come in steaming drunk, banging around and that. At the time I just needed my methadone and not an argument, so my attitude would have been stinking at that point. I would have been wanting my methadone, screaming for it and probably not getting it until I listened and that probably didn't go down too well.

I picked up a can of Lynx and sprayed it in my eyes. I don't think I was trying to blame myself, I was just spraying it all over my face. My dad and my little brother Mark rugby-tackled me, jumped on top of me and lay on top of my legs to stop me moving. I was wriggling around for five minutes but I eventually calmed down and then they let me up. I had wanted methadone, that's all I had wanted and I probably wasn't getting it as quick as I wanted. I swore at my mum so she gave me a right hook. It was the only time my mum has ever hit me like that, but she hooked me and it was definitely unforgettable, shall we say. Well deserved. It did make me think about my attitude. That's the one thing I remember from my very first time going abroad to Turkey.

I did reduce my methadone from 40ml a day to 15mls a day in that two-week period while I was in Turkey. But then I came back to the streets of Edinburgh. I was with my daughter's mum at the time and we went back to the house in Musselburgh. It was only a matter of time before the drugs were brought out.

I had brought maybe a half, no a quarter of a litre worth of methadone back with me. There was a lot anyway because I wasn't taking it and I'd begged my mum to let me keep it just in case. But I always knew I was going to sell it because I could, so I could get heroin.

I wasn't ready to stop at that point in time. I didn't believe that anyone was able to stop because I thought heroin killed you, so I wasn't even trying to stop. The methadone worked physically so I wasn't withdrawn, I felt healthy, but there was always a draw towards heroin and that night I sold methadone and got heroin. It was lucky I was jetlagged and I had friends around who were drinking. They wanted me to drink, but I was absolutely shattered and I just wanted to be on my own so I went to bed and fell asleep. The next day I went out and punted the methadone so I could get a few bags of heroin to do me that week.

And then I just went straight back to my old ways, and that was trying to source money to keep my addiction going. And that went on for years.

Chapter 11

Obviously my first ambition is to stop taking opiates. I'm not really ambitious but since my daughter was born that has changed. I'm the one that's supposed to be out there earning money, but I'm in so much debt that I would have to work for nothing. I don't always want to be a waster and hopefully if I stay off the drugs I'll be able to start thinking straight again. All I want is to be happy, but at the moment I'm not and I feel guilty because I have a daughter that I love very much but in my head I sometimes think that they would be better off without me and my drugs. I'm supposed to be writing about my ambitions but there is only my drug problem that takes up the space.

****

I wrote this while in a dark place. Suicide was on my mind and I didn't think I was getting out. I wrote that text as a message for once I was gone to let everyone know that the drugs had taken me. I have cried many times writing this book as I have to relive the memory in my head (and I'm welling up now). I wasn't finished and thankfully I didn't. I would have said goodbye as an ending and that may have pushed me over the edge. I couldn't go like that but what was going to happen?

I used a mirror to kick my heroin habit. It was Kyle's birthday. I woke up and stuck the kettle on. My pills were lined up as usual – six dihydrocodeine, a few Valium, and antidepressants too. Heroin was just an extra back when I finally managed to stop. Methadone, MSTs, Tramadol and codeine were my drugs of choice. Heroin was always difficult to get so these sorts of drugs were handy to keep me going. Anyway, I made my milky cup of tea and went into the living room. I'd made it milky so I could gulp my tablets, usually loaded with three sugars. On this morning, though, I finished my tea quickly and I hadn't followed my daily routine. The tablets were sitting on the table. I walked up to the big mirror I had and said to myself aggressively: 'Don't fucking ask for any more drugs because you're not getting any.'

I pushed my nose up to the glass and I felt a massive shiver down my spine, followed by the biggest goose bumps I've ever had. Shit, I'd done it, I'd beaten this addiction. I knew instantly I was clean. Last night heroin still in my veins, but now I knew I'd never touch it again. I remember being so happy and wanting to phone my mum. She would be at work but always answered my calls so this would be great news. If only I hadn't relapsed so many times. Nobody believed me and that was ok. I understood why.

My excitement was short-lived as the cramps took effect and I was shortly needing this drug. It was all physical withdrawals from that moment forward. I remember smiling as I sat and looked at my tablets. A text came asking if I wanted to go for a bag of smack. I said no money, sorry, as I knew that would get rid of them. The withdrawals were not nice, but compared to any other time it was easy. I knew I wasn't going to touch drugs so deal with it, I told myself.

After a week of being locked away I started to feel stronger and my appetite came back like I never thought would be possible. I ate and ate for months and it felt amazing. I would go to my mum's for a Sunday roast and usually leave it on the bunker, but now I was down every night ransacking the fridge and looking for desserts, too. I had told my parents at the Sunday roast that I'd stopped and I think they saw a difference in me. It would have to take time to build trust, but I just wanted to scream to everyone.

As the months passed it was clear to everyone I was getting better as the weight began to return to my face. I gave the tablets away to a friend and even took them to get a bag of heroin about a week after I got clean but that was a test. I was bigging myself up inside for doing it. I was offered a tooter more than once and I always said no. They hated I'd done it as I was a source of money for them, that's the reality, all friendships aside. Drugs are number one for every addict.

One song saved my life more than once and that was R.E.M.'s Everybody Hurts.

Chapter 12

My family can take all the credit for getting me clean of my heroin addiction. My mum and dad, my three brothers, my auntie and my uncle, and later my nieces, and eventually I had my very own beautiful baby girl. We are all very close and protective and it shocked them to the core to find out I was in massive trouble.

Heroin got the better of me because I was weak-minded and my friends were all smoking it. I was a gullible fool back then; I let them take me for a ride.

I was the main transport to get our fixes. Niddrie and Bingham were our destinations. If we didn't get it in one area, I drove to the next and then back and forth until we got our bags of heroin. Milky Bars and Kit Kats at hand, we would use the foil from one to make a tooter (silver tube) and another to chase the dragon.

It was easy to hide at first because I was working for four years of it. The tablets and methadone came later, but back at the start I could finance my drug use. I was smoking heroin in the toilets at Scottish Widows; the building was massive and I had picked certain jobs so I would deliver the mail around the building so that I could stop off at every toilet. I had my foil wrapped perfectly and a bag of heroin down my sock. Heroin stinks of rotten fish so I'm sure the cleaner suspected something was going on, but I never got caught once. How I'll never know, because not only was I in the toilet for hours I was melted all the time. Maybe they just thought I was tired.

Every evening was an adventure. We would go to get a bag about teatime, usually in groups of three or four. More often than not we would have to wait hours. I can remember being out for days at a time. We went nowhere until it arrived at one of the many dealers. We were out-of-towners with a lot of cash and we were severely taken advantage of. I was never bumped, but the amounts were ridiculous. A second and third trip would follow until we were all gouching.

I only once saw someone inject and that was enough for me. I'd never put a needle anywhere near my body, smoking it was bad enough! When I think back, I don't know how I've survived. No criminal record, never bumped or mugged. Stabbings and muggings every night. However, when you need a burn you will chance your arm. A very dangerous place. If it hadn't been for my car I'm sure it would have happened. As soon as we got anything we would sing and dance like kids in the car. We were so pleased, even if we got one bag to go around five mouths. It was just a relief to get it.

Chapter 13

****

The biggest worry that I have about detoxing is not being able to complete it. I can't stay on opiates any longer because it's destroying everything I have left. I no longer exercise on a regular basis and when I do I ache for days. Mentally, drug addiction has made me into a monster that has no problem hurting the people closest. Flying off the handle is something that I have a big problem with as I can't seem to help myself even when I am with my partner and daughter. I've hated myself for a few years now and don't want to be like that anymore. I hope that if I detox successfully then most of the hatred and anger will disappear. I know I'll never be the same but anything would be an improvement. Since being on methadone everything seems to have stabilised. And the way that I look and act have gotten better, but in my head I still feel the same and it's getting worse each day. I'm finished if I can't get off opiates because they are slowly killing everybody that is addicted and I definitely don't want to be addicted in ten years' time. If I am always going to be an addict then I choose to be addicted to something positive.

****

I wrote the above text more than ten years ago, when I was in a very different place, I am still addicted to opiates, but for a medical reason not a mental one. I am working on beating this addiction but need a solid plan to fix my back.

I'm not concerning myself with my addiction at the moment as I'm in a strong place right now. I need to try to help those less fortunate. It really becomes tiresome as those around you continue to be negative, but you keep on track and block those suggestions that you can't change. Everyone will see addiction in a different light depending on which addictions you have suffered from. It's usually those who struggle with it who will try to put you down. They don't want you getting better as it leaves them behind. If you care about them, then get yourself better and teach them how you did it. If it's your own method and nothing to do with anything I've mentioned then that doesn't matter. It's knowledge the same as mine and needs to be shared. Yes, people will judge you and maybe pity you but you will feel better inside.

The stigma attached to heroin is the reason why most don't want to come out into the public eye. Some will, though, and that will start the ball rolling.

I plan to ask ex-addicts across the country to team up and create a restructure of education. The videos I've done so far on social media are just a taste of what's to come. Me sitting with tin foil isn't something I've ever planned to do again, but if it helps educate others I will share.

I really hope all existing charities listen to my plan and get on board, regardless of how much wages they currently pay. All help for this cause is welcome. Piggy backing is key to our goal. We need to help each other and learn from past experiences, never give up!

We need to start learning from our mistakes and learning from other people's mistakes, personally and as a nation. I know I'm not the only one that sees what's going on. I will not go into politics but my charity will not get lost – the good people in this world will see what I'm trying to do and support me. If I give the wheel a big enough shunt it will carry itself. Big-hearted people pulling together. Communities, squaddies, local businesses, all on the same page. Homelessness must be abolished forever. I will put my sound business plan to the government and the super-rich of the country. If they can't write a blank cheque, I will travel to London and try my luck there. I will fly if need be but please don't make me. I hate travelling and we are wealthy enough to fix it ourselves.

The next time I'm suffering with my back, I'm not sure what will happen. I worry about my health a lot and in recent times I've been suffering in silence. I've had bouts of dizziness, sickness, stomach cramps and that's after my tablets. Stress probably caused most of it. I fear doctors so I chose to man up and hope it goes away.

Detoxing is easier when you're ready. If you're lucky enough you will only suffer physically for a week or so. Your mind will know you've kicked the habit. Even stopping heroin and changing to other medications is a victory, but you must not stop on methadone or tablets – these drugs will also eat away at your health.

I want to share my experience of antidepressants. I found them to be good at first but after a few weeks I was zombified. Feeling drunk every morning was no good and I felt dead, no emotions whatsoever. Antidepressants play their part for short-term use perhaps, but prolonging your grief isn't the answer, the same problems will be there when you stop and you may have added some new issues. Again, everyone is different and that's my take on them.

Alcohol has never been an addiction, but I know I can't drink anymore. I am too emotional and often cry or become angry. It's the worst addiction for me. Worse than heroin. I am so glad I never took to drinking heavily. I see the horror this drug inflicts on the nation. We can't stop people having fun and socialising, so we need to look at alternatives.

One addiction that has never been serious for me is gambling: with an addictive personality I suppose I was always going to be drawn to it. I had my first bet at 15 – 25p each way on a rank outsider at 50/1. If it had won I'd be rich, as led for the first few furlongs. I spent a lot of time studying the Racing Post and Teletext to try to find a system. I've had my fair share of big prize winners at the horses, but I never put a lot on so I could still gamble even if they were all losers.

The feeling was always the same regardless of how much I bet. I would scream at my horse to hurry up and it was a rush if it won. Slots were my real weakness, though. I just couldn't walk past them. My winnings often ended up in the fruit machine. Even recently, I was gambling a lot so that addiction has followed me through life.

When I was around 23, I collected my money from the post office and went to put my usual 50p on a horse. The race was delayed and I couldn't stop looking at the flashing lights. I got £10 in coins and one at a time put them in the machine – seven times I did that. I was still using heroin at that point. The walk home wasn't nice – I ran or at least jogged the mile or so home. When I arrived I went straight to my room and locked the door. My mum followed me upstairs. I opened the door, broke down in tears and confessed what I had done. I never played fruit machines again until many years later.

Drugs have always been my main concern so other addictions have often gone unnoticed – Xbox, cigarettes, gambling and even browsing social media. I use the same method to try to stop these addictions.

Chapter 14

****

Emotional times are upon you my friend, but fear not I'm sure we will both get through it. If I ever mention our conversations to each other, people think I'm mad! Who can blame them? It is a bit strange but it has its upsides, like the fact that I can now control you and make a better life for us. You drove me to heroin for a start and if I hadn't realised in time it would have killed us! 'Split personality' just sounds a bit mad to me, because we don't disagree on everything. The truth is, both sides of me have too much love and not enough trust. You have to make the most of a bad situation. If you gave up smoking then I could sort us out even more than I already have.

Eight months in the gym, and look what I have done to us. I know it came as a bit of a shock to you, but if we're going for a better life where you won't exist then I'm just going to keep going and going. I'll be ripped.

Almost there, big guy!

****

I knew I was made of stronger stuff than I've shown all my life. I'm now in total control of my mind and proving it every day when I get up motivated. Getting fit is my new drug of choice. I get so much more respect nowadays. It's amazing what putting a couple of stone of muscle does. It means I'm no longer a skinny wee runt. I walk with confidence and I think people are starting to notice.

People always told me to be proud when I got clean, but I always thought that I never could because I couldn't forgive myself for being there in the first place. I got hooked on heroin for five years of my life and on methadone for a further two years and god knows how many tablets. I had frequent thoughts of suicide and I couldn't see any way out of that misery until I decided to do it for my family and not myself. Strange, I know – most people will say you have to do it for yourself but I'm telling you otherwise. It does come, but doesn't have to be the focus of you getting clean.

Deep down you will hate yourself, so you will choose to punish yourself by getting more wasted and prolong your agony. There is always a way out. Trust me, I'm living proof.

I was eight and a half stone and looked like a skeleton. I'm now bang on my target weight of twelve stone and fighting fit. Thanks to the gym and a punch bag, my addiction has changed. I train four days a week and it's all new to me. Muscles popping out that I didn't know existed. What I am trying to say is there is hope and if you read how I achieved my goals then maybe you can do the same.

I will hopefully show you that it's you who makes the decisions in your life. Your subconscious mind will keep you there. Learn how to control it and it's only the physical withdrawal that stands between getting clean or not. I'm not saying that it's easy, but if you're honest you will know that it's your mind that sends you on a trek for a bag of heroin anytime. You will get put down all the time unless you take a hard look at yourself and realise you're a better person than you've let yourself become.

Your mind has three parts: conscious, subconscious and creative subconscious. We can all achieve our goals in life. If we want to change our lives for the better, we need to change some of the stored information.

Your subconscious stores everything we experience. To help you understand how your mind works, you have to put it into practice. Your conscious mind is the bit you're using as you read this and your subconscious is now storing what you are reading or seeing or hearing. That's why it's essential you keep all the negative people in your life at a distance. It is storing it so you can remember it, complete with what you feel about it. What you believe to be true about your experiences and yourself is stored as your reality.

Your creative subconscious has the job of making sure you act as you believe you are. They say it maintains sanity. It's hard to understand but it is there, I promise you. It's the most powerful part of your being. It will get you clean.

Music can have a massive influence on your life, too. Make sure the messages in the lyrics are positive ones. The little voice that tells you to pick your nose or go for a pee is an important wee guy; he is your mind. Pull him into line and focus on blocking the negative first as that's the life-threatening part. Use anything you can. I use happy memories that are always ready to block because it hurts when you're criticised. It's human nature that your first instinct will be anger or sadness. If I feel myself getting sad I listen to happy music, inspirational stories or exercise and it works every time.

You will get times of sadness and anger, but don't let them define you. Everyone has a heart and a mind, but we often rule by our hearts. There are ways to help you.

Dream big and keep dreaming big. Always have a Plan B, but follow your dreams. Don't let anybody tell you that you can't or you won't – life is yours to go out there and try your heart out at any stage of your life. We live in a world of wonders and you are never too old to change your life. We have all made mistakes, but we can make sure we use the time we have left helping our own lives.

Happiness is better than sadness, so you must change that. Because of my own guilt about my addiction I'm choosing to help the homeless, but you can do anything good and use it to keep you focused on the positive things in life, no matter how grim. Build on small victories, take the knocks on the chin and continue building happy memories. Leave negative people behind – they serve you no purpose. You are hopefully blocking them so they become 'nothing people'. Most will be lovely people, but be careful, some will not want you getting better and moving on.

Chapter 15

****

At last I can write down how I feel and not shed a tear. This is all new for me, and how good does it feel. There's only one place where I can start and that is going away on my course, because that is where I found the key to my happiness. It's taken me 26 years but at last I've made it. Yippee!

One door has closed and I'm throwing away the key; another has just opened and I'm melting it into my mind. I'm so happy and confident nowadays that I feel on top of the world. The world is my oyster and that's the way it's staying. My friends and family have stuck by me through all my problems and I'm so grateful. I will show them all how much I love them if it's the last thing I do. I'm special and I do have a heart of gold, so I think it's time to start shining.

There are so many people who helped me through my recovery, but I really think I should take most of the credit. It's so easy to relapse when things are going wrong, but I stayed strong and it paid off because I've turned into the person I should have been a long time ago. Drugs have obviously made a major impact on who I am, but if I can help people with my knowledge then it wasn't a complete waste of seven years.

****

I wrote this after returning from the Cyrenians course. The Cyrenians is a charity that runs courses for people who are having difficulties in life – problems at home or school, or problems with drugs – and it needs to be acknowledged by the government. That course was life-changing for me. It was not so much the group getting together or the games, but the teaching day. An American professor explained how your mind works and I actually understood what he was meaning. This voice in my head is my mind. Oh, wow! And you can change it, this is getting better. The power of positive thinking and the dangers of negative thinking, too. How you store certain emotions and images.

I realised the negative feelings I was getting could be controlled. Back then I didn't think it was going to work. I'd met a girl on the course and that was going to help my mood. She was lovely, but I met her on a course for people with similar issues so it was a testing time.

I remember smoking grass and thinking about the professor's teachings. I had music on and as I was listening to the lyrics I realised the messages from the voices I love were impacting my mood. Then I applied what had I learned and blocked all the sad or negative lyrics. I only focused on happy messages; even in sad-sounding songs there are many positive messages. I took the emotions into my heart and felt relief. Happy, happy, happy. Block everything else.

Chapter 16

****

It's July 2008 and we have just had six weeks of rain, which annoyed me like you wouldn't believe because I'm a sun-seeker, and when I woke up this morning there wasn't a cloud in sight. So I grabbed my shades and my music box and lay in my back garden at ten o'clock. Then I started to plan my day ahead. I'll be down the beach shortly. I think my bag is already packed to go to the gym, but not on a day like this.

Ever since my back acne four years ago I've needed the sun to help it heal. There's nothing I can do about the scars but getting a tan helps a lot. I remember the times when I would not take my top off. I hated it when the sun was shining and I had to keep covered up. Changed days now, I don't care what people think. My neighbours tell me I live a life of luxury because I'm always sunbathing morning, noon or night. At seven o'clock at night I'll still be in my garden soaking up the rays. I get a few funny looks when I'm lying out in the morning. We live in Scotland so I will be taking advantage of every minute it's sunny.

****

I suffered from severe back acne. It was caused by a mixture of bad diet and drugs intake, I reckon. The boils would be huge and angry.

I used to go out for a few drinks with my friends, they always bought me drinks. Some bought me food, too. I was a bit of a scrounger. I was on Jobseeker's Allowance and my £56 a week didn't go far. I lived alone and I had bills to pay and a drug habit to pay for. I would have £10 at the start of the night, I'd go out and get drunk and take amphetamines and still have enough for a hamburger chip roll on the way home. If I didn't my mates would have bought me one. I loved how they looked out for me,

I remember growing with confidence as I was in the gym and on protein shakes. I saw a small difference so decided to put a tight white dress shirt on to show I was getting better. It was more for my own sanity as confidence was always an issue.

I only write when I'm stoned and draw when I'm happy. It annoys me to write words I don't mean to. I hope to stop smoking soon for health and fitness reasons, also to relax although my anxiety has eased a bit. But it helps me because I'm on my own. Violins, please! It's true though I often admit to being lonely, but it's thankfully through choice. Trust has been non-existent since splitting with my daughter's mother but when I meet the right girl I'll know and it will be all good. In the meantime, I'm going to keep training.

I think I've proved everyone wrong again. The first time was when people doubted me over getting clean and more recently that I would not stick to the gym. I've trained four days a week for four hours, a session including swimming and cycling on my days off. Put on a much-needed three and a half stone of muscle. Four years ago I was eight and a half stone so my appetite went through the roof. I soon achieved ten stone, but didn't train so much back then so it felt good having a chest and gut. I hit my target of twelve stone last month. I was over the moon, jumping off the scales like a loony in the gym. I'm happy with the way things are heading now. Healthy body and mind. Lucky man!

****

I wrote that at the age of 27. Weight has always been an issue for me. The time I remember most was sitting in the doctor's. He asked me to make a food diary as my weight was dropping quickly. Basically, a typical day was a stupid amount of tea loaded with three sugars, lunch would be flaming hot Monster Munch with thirty-three per cent extra crisps and two heavily buttered rolls, chocolate for my tea as it took away the hunger pangs. I lasted about a month. The doctor said: 'Paul, heroin won't kill you but your malnutrition will.'

I started protein shakes from that day and stopped losing weight. There was a lot of physical pain to get to where I was, but it was all worth every second. Nothing good ever comes easy. Shakes were a saviour for me while I was in training. I couldn't afford the food I craved so used those to keep my hunger at bay. Drugs were more important than my health. I often starved and sat in the freezing cold just so I could afford opiates.

Chapter 17

There was a route I'd found round Arthur's Seat that confirmed what I thought. I'm mental when it comes to cycling downhill. I always take the most difficult routes when it's possible. One night, for instance, I went up a steeper incline and if I stopped I struggled to get going again, so I just attacked every slope. To my surprise I made it to the base of the final ascent to the top. You can't take your bike unless you carry it; all the steps are a mission in themselves. I always have a rest and admire the view. Scotland is such a beautiful country and being away up there lets me see Edinburgh in a different light.

On the way down is where the fun starts. I'd found this route by accident and it really gets the adrenaline going. It starts as a small slope uphill until it levels out, but you can notice the difference in the ground. There are boulders that must be jumped and gravel that's slightly unsteady, so my balance can't be all that bad. I jumped them with ease and turned the corner, which is terrifying because the path slopes down and becomes very steep. Great view, though. Suddenly I found myself pulling both brakes and failing to stop the bike; my back brake works fine but the front plays up a lot. That night it was not the night for brake failure. I came flying down the side of Arthur's Seat and almost ended up in the pond. I was doing about 25 mph as it was downhill. An ambulance turned up and checked me over. I got a lecture for not wearing a helmet and was sent on my way. I was black and blue when I got home.

In those days I was becoming a bit of an adrenaline junkie. Arthur's Seat is a very dangerous place, but I felt I could climb a good part of it. I did on several occasions, but it was pure stupidity. I remember being in some pretty dodgy situations up there, hanging from places I had no right to be in, gathering an audience a few times, It was just another addiction, when I think back. The more people watching, the more daring I would become. I loved the attention, I suppose, and I was extremely fit back then. The army would soon be upon me, so my mindset back then was 'better get training'.

I had to prove something to all the doubters. I'd been clean for years so it was time to take the next big step and change my job prospects, I asked for the fire brigade application form first, but when I looked at the huge amount of paperwork I thought, 'Nah, no thanks'.

Portobello beach was my favourite place. It was an amazing place to grow up. As a kid I spent every summer there. There were amusement arcades and Nessie the rollercoaster. The sand was great but the water was cold. My later memories of Portobello beach were tarnished, as I'd started my addiction to heroin there. But as I recovered, I put that right.

I realised weighted runs in boots was something the army would want so I practised round Arthur's Seat and on the heavy beach sand. Shades on, headphones in, I was away all day and each time it became easier and easier.

Thankfully, I'm back to loving Portobello beach again. I was always sunbathing for my bad skin and I could spend days sitting there dreaming. Dreaming turned out to be planning. I have been planning all these years. 'Follow your planning' doesn't sound right, though, so we will stick with dreams,

One night I went out for a few pints and ended up wanting to fight with a bouncer. I had a better chance against the bouncer, even though he was twice the size of me. It's not necessarily the size of the dog in the fight, but the size of the fight in the dog and for that reason I gave myself a fighting chance against him. But the fight never happened, so I kicked a metal pole instead and there could be only one outcome against metal. I fractured my foot.

I should really practise what I preach and learn from my mistakes. I'd had a fight with concrete a couple of years previously and fractured my hand. I'd been sitting in the sun all day and not eaten anything, then I went out at five o'clock. I can't handle my alcohol at the best of times, It's a recipe for disaster. For example, I'll feel tipsy after half a can of lager. I don't drink spirits anymore because it blows my mind. Cider and snakebites are my drink when I go out. I still get pissed but I'm more in control without spirits.

The fractured foot meant I was out for six to eight weeks. I'd been training four days a week for nine months and was toning my six-pack. I was cycling everywhere and generally liking my life.

Then I got an infection in my left testicle that even after five months was not shifting, but getting worse. I was scared shitless. I wanted to start Muay Thai again but I couldn't until both my foot and testicle had healed. I had even had to stop boxing and I was pissed off about that big time as it was a good release for my anger and kept me fit. I couldn't wait to get to the gym as I could still lift weights but it was expensive having to get the bus there as I no longer had my driving licence. I was still motivated even though it would have been easier to rest. I was scared that if I stopped, I wouldn't start again and I'd lose all my hard work. I was making them both worse by training and working.

However, I got signed off and was able to sort out my workouts. My foot eventually healed totally and I went back to training hard. I had lost my six-pack but it began to reappear and my confidence grew when I looked in the mirror. I felt I looked hot, so I just needed to stop being so off-putting to the chicks.

I went for an ultrasound on my testicles to check for cancer. I was still in a lot of pain and worried because nobody knew what was up with me. I hoped to find out the following week at the hospital. My doctor suggested it might be a deep tendon tear because of all the training. It was possible but it was still not healing and my ball was definitely sore. I didn't want to stop training as I was still scared I wouldn't start again.

Chapter 18

I had gone back to work after recovering from my addiction. I always found it difficult coping with money and I'd let things get out of control. Thanks to my heroin addiction, I owed £15,000 to banks and sharks. I'm only paying money from my wages to the council, which was £20 a month when it was meant to be £70. I messed up with the paperwork again and this time it could see me out in the streets.

I'd trained my mind so well to ignore negative things in my life by now that letters didn't register anything. I just saw bad things happening. If I let anything depress me just now, I'd have had it. Hopefully I could sort some of the mess out now. I needed this house because my daughter was going to need a home and I was going to provide one.

What was once a prison is now a haven. It took a long time to accept that my daughter didn't live here anymore, but she will be back. I often asked myself if I would be as strong if I didn't have my daughter to think about. The honest answer is, I doubt it. I would still be clean of drugs, but thinking of her helped me to train hard. I needed to be fit to protect my family. If anybody hurt my family, then they would answer to me. I'm sure my brothers felt the same. We are a close family and I love it. We are all over-protective over the things we love.

Ever since I was a wee boy in primary school, I've had the gift of making people laugh and it was only just coming back to me after a stint of depression. I can pull the most ridiculous faces. At school I always acted like a clown – it seemed to fit my nature the best. I was always popular, but never respected. My big brother got all the respect and I hated that, but I learned to live with it. Even my little brother picked up on it, which caused a lot of fights. My big bro would belt me, so I would belt my wee bro for laughing and he always whacked me right back. I used to think how unfair that was that I got hit twice. My youngest bro Kyle got it from Mark as well so I would stick up for him only to get kicked by them both. How's that fair?

****

Boggie boys have always been the best

So long been a trio and I've been a pest

But since I've got better my tongue needs a rest

We all have brains but now also muscles

Fair enough, we had loads of tussles

But this band of brothers will never be broken

A great gift from our parents, such a great token

If I was to cry tears of love, yous would all be soaken

We will always stick together and never lose touch

Because we love each other so very much

The strong stuff we are made of is clear to see

Just check out our muscles, including me, hee hee!

So Boggie boys let's have a happy Xmas and all be merry

If I'm having a drink it's Lambrini and it's got to be cherry

****

I found making people laugh helped me to be happy. Two decades later I still felt the same. Sometimes I thought the only way I'd get the respect I wanted was by going out and kicking some ass. It was just not in my nature but I felt the boxing training would make me more than capable of decking people in my life who disrespected me. I always rose above violence even when it made me look like a coward. I used to be a coward but it was most definitely not the case now.

I should have engaged with the boxing when I was young, I had very little football skills, especially compared to those two lanky shits Mark and Kyle. That was another thing. How did I end up being a short arse? Kevin was even shorter though. I'm not bitter but I'll always remember the sly kicks just because Kevin was there. All my brothers have a sense of humour – the younger ones, anyway. Kyle is jokebook daft and Mark just acts daft, but is funny with it. Luckily, they never had the same issues with drugs; me and Kevin were just the bad boys growing up.

When you're a sheep you end up in some pretty dodgy situations. I always felt like a sheep until I finished the course at the Cyrenians. Everyone thought they were boxers or martial artists growing up. It turned out we were really just training our whole lives; without toy fighting you wouldn't learn what works. I know every place on my body that's sore when kicked, punched, stomped, or even suplexed.

I was still training in the gym four days a week and working part-time so I could stay off the dole. My boxing seemed to be coming along too. I just needed to concentrate harder. Attractive women often caught my eye and imagination. Boxing was a great release for me and my anger. I would pound a heavy bag for an hour every day and I leave my gym feeling happy and it lasted. I'd never been in a ring but I thought it was close. I was good at it but I feared someone would beat me up – fear keeps you alive! For now I was going to continue training hard and maybe I might would be pleasantly surprised. Sometimes I felt like Bruce Lee. I would overcome my fear. I found it easy to mimic people. I'd always liked Chris Eubank's stance and that seemed to suit me comfortably. My stance was not as good obviously, but I was getting there.

I tried the body combat class at my gym. It was good and the women were attractive. I expected to see at least a few guys, but I was alone with eight hot chicks! I noticed a big difference in the way I was moving now. All this training was starting to pay off. I could hit harder, faster and for longer than I'd ever been able to do. It came as a bit of a surprise when the instructor thought I was a martial artist. I laughed because positive feedback made me feel alive. I knew the girls were watching me so I tried my best. I'd also been to a few Muay Thai classes, which taught me respect and a few moves.

I wanted to learn to dance properly. Don't get me wrong – I could shake my ass with the best of them, but I thought I was good at it and it would keep me fit. I thought if I combined dancing and boxing I could be good enough to practise both. My instructor said I looked like I'd studied martial arts. I was just mucking around on the heavy bag in the dance studio so she was shocked to find that I'd had only a few lessons in Muay Thai and boxing.

There was life in the old dog yet. I was a mess for seven years but I'd proven that drugs were not going to get the better of me. Everybody had accepted that I was not a waster. The muscle I'd put on probably helped, but my mindset could take all the credit. I'd told myself I'd get off heroin, that I would put on three and a half stone and that I'd train hard at the gym. I'd now been clean for four years and hit my weight target of twelve stone. I ate and ate till my stomach couldn't handle it and I trained for nine months.

I just had to work out how my mind worked. Being positive was the key. I used to take my phone to see what I looked like, and I had some speed for an old dog. All those weighted runs round Arthur Seat paid off. I could feel my skinny wee legs struggling with the weight, but I kept going. I had shin splints for a while but muscles were developing that I never knew were there. I could open up running flat out and it got easier and easier. I had always smoked but it never hampered me like I thought it would. I knew it was bad for me, but I was so active that my lungs were stronger.

I still acted shy but my confidence was growing with my muscles, so that was improving also. I used to hate myself deep down and it was only a matter of time before something snapped. Even though I felt like that I'd managed to fool everyone. People laughing always made me feel so happy, so I became a bit of a clown at school. Now, the only thing that had changed was that I didn't hate myself anymore. 'Love myself' was a tad too much, but I was getting there. A positive attitude was key to my whole life. Onwards and upwards.

I'd changed so much for the better in the last year. I was happy almost every day and it felt great. Don't get me wrong – I still had issues but compared to where I was I thought I'd achieved a hell of a lot.

From heroin to hero, I try to pick my words carefully. Granted, hero is a bit strong but you have to big yourself up every now and then.

Chapter 19

I was 30 when I joined the army and older than almost everyone. I was really nervous about my first fitness test. It was like sports day at school, only there were forty men going for a one and a half mile race. I'd put the work in so I wouldn't be last. We took off and I went straight up front, to the amusement of everyone else.

'Ha ha! Look at Boggie, the auld bastard, he is going to fail.'

I felt that comment in my heart and I came in second that day. We lined up with our time and when the PTI came along you told him your time. The PTI looked at me and laughed.

'How old are you, FFS?'

'Thirty, Staff,' I replied.

He nodded at me and moved on. From that day I noticed a change in respect from everyone in training and all ranks. If I was going to do well, I reckoned it would only be my fitness that would save me. I was even better with weight on my back and I showed a lot of men up. Anything fitness, I was in. My fear that 18-year-old whippersnappers would run rings around me was over. Even the fittest of men always had me on their heels. All the boys were brilliant during training. It was the hardest thing I would ever achieve in life and coming from me that is something (this book comes second, maybe).

Drill was something else. I'd watched videos and I was very impressed with the Guards. I soon found out I was going to struggle, though. That was what set us apart and it would be my downfall. I just couldn't get it. Old dogs and new tricks were mentioned. I did always try, but my body just didn't like it. It took me a long time to learn and I almost got back-squadded for it. On one occasion I turned and my partner halted. It didn't go well for me as it was an important inspection, and I'd only just picked it up, too. I overheard someone saying 'Boggie's getting back-squadded', and I marched back to my room heartbroken. All that hard work and it was over. I pulled my feet in and confessed how upset I was. I shed a tear – I'm a passionate, emotional man. I was not ashamed of it as I knew what it meant to continue. My mindframe during training was that if my friends got hurt, I'd pick them up. I was the fittest in our section and obviously the oldest, so it was up to me I felt.

A few days into basic training we had a drill rehearsal. We were practising attaching bayonets and it wasn't too bad compared to some other drill movements, but I wouldn't escape the drama that always seemed to unfold when I practised my drill. I was picking it up nicely, but on our final try I cut my ear with the bayonet, please don't ask me how. We were in three ranks and I felt the blood drip down my ear. What should I do? I decided to move my hand to my ear. It didn't go down well.

'Trainee Guardsman Boggie! WHY ARE YOU MOVING ON PARADE?'

'I've cut my ear, Sergeant,' I replied.

The sergeant wasn't pleased and tore me a new arsehole on the drill square. I was so embarrassed. Later he came to see me and noticed the gash in my ear. He was understanding, but explained why I should never move.

Loaded marches were my favourite. I have skinny wee legs as well, which always confused me. I could carry the biggest of men with all their kit on and I proved it one day in training. Thankfully all ranks were there that day and it didn't go unnoticed. I was getting a reputation for being a fitness freak.

I hate wasps with a passion and the next few times they put me to the test. I remember one was buzzing around and the sergeant was shouting to ignore it. It landed on me and started to tickle my face with its legs. I did not move once and it finally flew on, but left the most annoying itch. Have you ever tried to ignore an unbearable itch? It's totally alien, every part of your being wants to scratch it.

On one occasion during training, we were in our room ironing our uniforms when a sergeant from another platoon walked in. We were all petrified and stood to attention. He walked around the room and took the piss out of all the guys, then he arrived at me. He had obviously seen my fitness test results; he also knew my drug past.

'How are you, Boggie?' he asked.

'Good, Sergeant. Thank you,' I replied.

From that moment on he had my back all through training and although he wasn't with our platoon he often checked in on me, also out in the field.

Some sergeants didn't take kindly to my cheek. It was always at times when we were having a laugh, but I gave as good as I got. Most of my peers respected me. I would always try my heart out even if I wasn't great at it. It was my recovery from heroin that most amazed me and my fitness was unreal back then. I had found a new addiction and I was hooked. I'd train all the time even when we had downtime and I usually burned myself out being so keen to prove everyone wrong,

We went to France on an exercise with the French Airborne; it wasn't very nice but part of our training. I was put in the lance corporals section. We took orders and were told that if we ever hit a metalled road we had gone too far. Two hours in and we did indeed hit a metalled road.

'Corporal, we have gone too far,' I said.

'You all stay here and I'm going to check the other side of that hill.'

It was miles away. We got our scoff out and made a brew, watching in disbelief as the corporal disappeared into the distance. I was a whinge-bag at times and this didn't go down well with me, but you always respect rank. Heavy rain started falling and we were quickly soaked through. Eventually the corporal returned and we marched on for another hour or so before we came to a river. The whole platoon was waiting on us. We were, of course, on the wrong side.

'How the hell did you manage that, you stupid arses?' the sergeant asked.

I stayed quiet as I was soaked and fuming. There was a safe crossing a few miles downriver, or we could cross the deep bit. It was clear the guys didn't want to cross, but I was pissed off and after sorting my kit I jumped straight into the river to everyone's amusement.

'Are you crazy,' asked the sergeant major.

'No, Sir, I'm just annoyed,' I replied.

'Go get yourself dried off and get some warm food in you,' he replied.

The following day we went out on patrol. I wasn't the best map reader, but I knew enough. I also had eyes. We walked round in circles for hours, seeing the same tree with a unique yellow foliage. I moaned that we had already been that way. Luckily the corporal and

I got on, so he just told me to shut up. Eventually night fell and we came to a stop. It was freezing. Everyone had icicles on their noses and it was clear we were suffering. I asked if I could get my gas canister out to heat my hands, but it was a tactical exercise so I wasn't even able to smoke, or burst into flames as it was called in the army.

The basic training was the hardest physical training I've ever done. I was always freezing or soaked, but I loved it. I was a soldier for real and tried not to moan too much. Morale is important so I took to being a joker to ease our suffering. Having a laugh made it easier though.

Ceremonial duties in London were getting closer, but I hadn't passed out yet and I still didn't think I'd get to the end. Injuries came and went and I was still getting stronger. I remember waiting to go onto the drill square one day for passing out parade rehearsals. I had just watched Braveheart and remembered the words of William Wallace. 'Sons of Scotland, I am Paul Boggie and I see a whole army of my countrymen.' That caused a bit of a commotion as we were full of English, Welsh and Irish so there were a few boos, but mostly laughter and cheers. It was just to pass the time and help us to relax as we were all in the same boat.

All of us were absolutely shattered. We'd be up all week digging trenches or bulling boots, it was all go all the time. I often slept in the chair after scoff, to the amusement of everyone else. Auld man Boggie needed his power nap.

When you don't think you're going to get any further than basic training and suddenly you're standing ready to go on your passing out parade, and all your family are there along with all the other boys. It was a big deal. I almost got the Best Physical Training award, which I felt I deserved but I'm not bitter … much.

I had done all my lockers, my boots were bulled like glass, my ablutions were spotless and I was ready to step off. I had a problem with the stitching in my tweeds. Why me? I was given a green belt to put on, which took the strain off the stitching, which was coming apart. As we stepped off and round the drill square to the cheers of the crowd, we were brought to attention and the stitching burst completely. I was left standing there, my tweeds only held together by the green belt. The more commands I followed, the more I could feel them drop. 'Just don't come down,' I told myself. I managed to get through it – it had taken my mind off what I'd actually just done. I was going to London.

I was in disbelief at passing out. How had I passed basic training? Hard work, hard work, hard work. My rifle skills were average, although my shot wasn't bad if I zeroed my rifle in properly. I practised, but it was clear I was a bit slower than most at taking things on board. I was a massive joker the whole time, but I did try when it came to drill and skill at arms training. I often heard morale mentioned in connection to me and I liked that. It upset some folk, but the majority had nice things to say about me. I enjoyed it when the boys were all laughing, so I would sit them all down and tell them of my days smoking heroin and taking other drugs.

Chapter 20

I'd never been to London and this was getting real now. I was nervous as my drill wasn't the greatest but what an honour to do this. On arrival in London we got a bit of downtime and often spent it having a beer. Sylvester Stallone had just left the barracks after meeting some of the guys the week before. I think he'd been in London for The Expendables. Maybe the guys would still be there when I got there, but no, they were away.

London was amazing. Being a Guardsman in London comes with the usual responsibility to conduct yourself properly. You also are respected a lot more by the police. I had hidden from the police my whole life, but here I was being respected by them, and they were armed. I got mistaken for higher ranks a lot in public. Folk would automatically assume I was a sergeant or PTI because I was so old and fighting fit.

I often kept the boys in line when we were out on the piss, as I knew everyone would be looking at me to be responsible. I did try but alcohol started to take over a bit. It's not an addiction, it was stress. I knew I could just stop drinking, but I was getting worried. I'd looked at the details and my first posting would be to Windsor Castle the following week. Right, let's see, I know the commands… but I was shit scared to be honest. This was massive for me and drinking only helped in the short term. I would end up on whisky and I'm bad on spirits so I needed to calm down and focus on Windsor Castle. I watched some videos on YouTube and started to relax, telling myself to just pay attention.

The day came and I was nervous even though I'd been running the last few days to help destress myself. My time came to march outside. The sun was on my face, it was July and roasting: this was going to be tough. Bearskin, tunic and rifle, and we stepped off. I was posted at the furthest away point and as I was posted, I was told how many steps to take either side. I didn't catch my instructions right and rather than say anything I just stood there, listening to the footsteps fade into the distance.

I realised Her Majesty might bring the dogs out with this fresh lemonade I'd heard about. You would think I'd be excited, but that made me worse. I didn't know how many steps to take so I decided to stand still the full time I was there. Her Majesty never showed but I didn't mind, it was probably for the best. I'd done it and nobody will ever be able to take that from me. I was so proud of myself.

When I got back it felt amazing to take my bearskin off. I was drenched in sweat. I have great memories of all the places in London I guarded. Buckingham Palace was like you were a popstar, cameras flashing constantly. That's the moment I remember when thinking about my heroin days and the feeling of pride is still with me today. Not everyone gets an opportunity like that and I grabbed it with both hands.

The ceremony of the keys at the Tower of London was another 'OMG' moment.

'Halt! Who goes there?' I bellowed.

I was in disbelief much of the time; these places and people were a whole different world and it was daunting to say the least. I had truly turned my life around, and thoughts of going to war were becoming frequent: 'It's what I was trained to do so let's put it into practice.' I was scared for a couple of months and spoke to nobody of this. One night the boys paid me a visit and started joking about us going to war. I soon realised they had my back and I had theirs so the fear subsided and then turned to excitement.

Chapter 21

I had decided I would try everything I could once I'd joined the army. I would get to see the world from a different perspective and that would surely broaden my mind. While I was in London, an opportunity came up to go sailing on the Gladeye yacht. I put my name forward even though I didn't fancy it much. Who knows, I may have loved it but I'd never find out unless I tried.

Names were dropped in a bowl and guess whose name came out first... You guessed it, I was going sailing for a week to France.

We drove down to Portsmouth. I thought it was amazing, Docked and ready to board, we jumped on and got a crash course in the dos and don'ts of sailing. There are lots of moving parts on a yacht and it wasn't easy to remember them all. Everyone else had been on a yacht before and understood what to do. I was unsure, but knew I'd pick it up quickly by watching everyone else.

That night we had food then went for a pint; a few of us moved onto a nightclub for some shots but we were up first thing. I'd had one too many and the following morning it didn't go down well. The waves as we tried to cross the Channel were horrendous, throwing us all to and fro. I was green and quickly threw up, then I rushed downstairs and wrapped my legs around the base of the toilet. If I didn't I was getting thrown all over the toilet so I hung on for dear life. The captain came down and said: 'Boggie, you're needed upstairs.' I just looked at him and he shouted: 'Boggie, isn't making it.'

I got a hard time once we returned to Portsmouth. It was deserved so I took it on the chin. The following morning we left again, but this time I was sober and the sea was calmer. Crossing open water is an amazing feeling; I quickly got to grips with sailing and enjoyed it so much (other than the storms, of course). We were a few hours away from France so I decided to go have a sleep up top. I lay down at the front of the yacht over the sail and stuck Paolo Nutini on my phone. I eventually nodded off, but when I opened my eyes the yacht was under water! The sea was white and frothy, so I grabbed any rope I could, not caring if it was a 'don't touch' rope. I just freaked out.

When I looked up they were all standing with their cameras at the ready, laughing and taking pics. I shouted: 'What was that?' They pointed to a huge container ship passing in the distance. They had clocked it and knew the bow wave would throw us up in the air a bit. They thought it was funny to leave me sleeping, but I could have lost my phone so cheers, guys. Payback for getting drunk on the first night, maybe. I honestly thought we were in serious trouble.

Arriving in France was a culture shock. Nobody in the streets and the shops were all closed. I just wanted a pint, but everywhere was shut. I walked and walked until I found a wee bar, though. 'Bonjour, une grande bière,' I said, and I finally got a pint.

The guys were a good laugh and enjoyed a pint too, so we spent a lot of time drinking. I've never drunk so much as when I was in London. Drugs were always my thing, but I couldn't go back there. Sailing and drinking don't mix either, especially on rough seas. I'm glad I went sailing as it was a great life experience.

Skiing was something I didn't fancy much growing up. I'd much rather sit or lie down on a sled, but we were going to the French Alps with the army and I'd survived sailing so bring it on, I thought, how hard can it be? I've watched the Olympics. Travelling on a coach wasn't too bad but the ferry was a bit choppy, shall we say. The food court was jammed with people trying to run to their seats before we got thrown around again. I just looked for a seat and never moved. It was only a few months back that we'd gone sailing so I could remember the feeling when the waves started.

We all got a briefing at the start and it wasn't long before everyone was hitting the slopes. I chose to go for a pint instead as a few of the boys didn't know how to ski either. We were to be up at 7am for our first lesson on the baby slopes. I did have an issue with drinking, but not a serious one. I drank out of boredom, I think.

I ended up missing my lesson as I was too drunk so I went for a swim instead. I got a ticking off for that and was banned from drinking the rest of the trip. It did me a favour, if I'm honest. The following day the guys were moving up the slopes as they had picked it up the first day. The instructor didn't like my attitude about drinking and I understood what he was saying. I could not ski. Period. So I was on my arse all day, but let's take Boggie higher up.

We ended up going to the top – to this day I'll never understand why I was up that high even as an amateur.

I was supposed to get a lift down, but we missed the closing time because I couldn't keep up. The weather changed in the space of ten minutes and it was getting dark. The snow was so thick. I couldn't see, so I just followed the instructor. We ended up having to radio for a snowmobile to get me. The French boy wasn't pleased and I swear he went full throttle down the side of that mountain. At one point I was coming off, but managed to grab the rails. When we arrived at the bottom, I said 'Merci, mon pute', which I thought was 'thank you, my friend', but turned out to be 'thank you, my whore'.

Pardon my French, but I had been using that same sentence all week thinking I was being friendly to every French person I spoke to. I was teaching the boys my new French words too.

I enjoyed going to France but I definitely won't be skiing again. I'd tried it and that's all that matters. Adventure training is an amazing experience for everyone. We were just a big, organised gang, I often thought. All ranks have a sense of humour, but you have to be careful not to overdo it or pick the times to joke about. I found if you're respectful in general then people mostly return it.

Chapter 22

When I was told that I was going to Canada, my first feeling was excitement as one of the main reasons for my joining the army was so that I could see a bit of the world. However, once I'd had a chance to speak to a few of the lads who had been before my excitement soon turned to dread. They said it was freezing even in the summer months and nothing but flat land for miles upon miles. This was going to be horrible, I thought. Anyway, I was going and I didn't have a choice in the matter.

The list came up for adventure training a week before deployment. I had a pick of several packages that I could go on: skydiving; white water rafting; ice climbing; rock climbing; canoeing; and horse riding. I've never seen the point of jumping out a perfectly good working plane, so skydiving was out even though it sounded the most adrenaline-filled. I'd never been that keen on water or heights either, so that left horse riding (rough ride). I'd never been on a horse, but how hard could it be? It was decided I was going horse riding for my first week in Canada.

After a nine-hour flight that seemed so much longer, I arrived at the ranch late in the afternoon but there was enough time to meet the cowboys or wranglers – I'm not sure which, but they seemed like a nice bunch of guys. After a few briefs about bears and snakes it was time to hit the hay. As usual it was an early start, something I'm used to so there was no problem there. Head cowboy Grant met us first thing and showed us how to prepare a horse for riding. First, he got two brushes and started brushing the horse, which seemed easy enough to me. Then you had to clear the horseshoes of mud and stones, so the horse would be in no discomfort. Then you put the blanket on followed by the saddle. Easy peasy, how difficult could it be? Well, of course, Grant was brought up with horses, so he did make it look easy.

When it was my turn to get up close to a horse, I was a wee bit nervous but I cracked on and managed to do what was shown to me. Next, we went to meet the horses we were going to be riding. The cowboys picked them for us and we had to go into the pen and fetch them. Thirty horses were running around and they wanted me to go inside. No way! I slipped to the back of the queue, so that there were only a few come my turn. As I walked into the pen, Grant shouted: 'Paul, you're on Smash!'

Smash was a grey horse that was stood in the corner gnawing on a wooden post. As I approached she turned her head and looked at me, then carried on gnawing. As I got to her she thought it would be funny to start walking away from me, much to the amusement of everyone watching. Grant came over and blocked her so that I could get the rope round her and head over to where she would be saddled. The first job was brushing, which I thought was the easiest job. I collected my brushes then headed back to Smash, who was now gnawing on a different post. I brushed her left side with no problems, then moved round to her right. I had watched The Horse Whisperer and seen how he could talk to them, so as I came round to the right side I whispered in her ear.

'Good, Smash. I hope you're going to be a good girl for me.'

As I started to brush under her stomach, as shown, I felt the sharpest pain on the side of my body. Smash had sunk in her massive teeth into me. I yelped in pain and jumped out the way. Grant came running over to find out what happened. I showed him the teeth marks and he started yelling at the horse. He grabbed the brushes out my hand and made his way towards Smash. As he slapped the brush across her neck she reared up and started kicking out, catching the horse next to her square on the leg. Eventually Grant showed me the two brushes and said: 'She won't bite you again!' I was thinking to myself, you've just made my horse go crazy and now you want me to ride her.

There were no other horses, so there was no choice but to ride Smash. I thought how she got her name – surely Nibbles or Crunch would be more appropriate. After a lot of help from the cowboys I managed to get a saddle on her, the problem now being how did I get on. Each time I put my foot anywhere near the stirrup she decided to walk off again. I had to rely on the cowboys.

Eventually we set off for a day's riding to get used to it. I soon discovered I was no jockey. We followed a trail through the forest where horses had obviously been going so it was quite easy. I just sat there holding the reins and let my horse follow the horse in front, single file. However, I was on a stubborn mule and it soon became apparent why she was called Smash.

I was at the back trotting along when we came to a fallen tree. Every other horse in front of me managed to step over it but not Smash. She decided to go round it and take me with her. At the last minute she would nudge to the side banging my knees off the trees as she went, smashing me left and right as she pleased. Then as we were getting back on the trail she decided to stop and go round in circles on the spot. I shouted at her and kicked her stomach with my heels. That didn't work. She began stamping her front right foot in the mud like a raging bull. After about twenty minutes of me shouting and her spinning and stamping, she got bored and decided to catch up with the rest of them at double speed. She almost threw me off at every turn and, of course, threw me into trees as she went. I just hung on for dear life and hoped I wouldn't fall. We caught the others up in no time and carried on along the trail. Day one finally came to a close and I was in no mood to brush down this horrible beast, but it had to be done – thankfully without any biting.

Day two would be different. I would get two carrots from the chef and the rest would be forgotten, I and Smash would become one. Who was I trying to kid? She never ate the carrots and tried to bite me twice as I put the saddle on. This was going to be an emotional journey into the Rockies. As I grew more confident after several river crossings and hills you wouldn't believe, I started to relax and so did Smash. The views were like nothing I had ever seen before – the north of Scotland on a massive scale is the only way to describe it, only they have bears and we have sheep. Over the next few days we covered many miles and took in some fantastic scenery. Although I never wanted to ride another horse as long as I lived I was grateful for the opportunity and made the most of it.

Exercises were about to start and the fact that it was happening two days early did not help morale. We all knew it was going to be tough for the first few days as you get used to being dirty, eating ration packs and stagging on the Warriors at 3 a.m. However, I found myself coping better than I had expected. The ration packs weren't bad, especially if you were hungry and it wasn't cold so when you got woken up for stag (sentry duty). It wasn't too bad and as for being dirty, everyone was in the same boat, or Warrior if you like, so the smell was hardly noticeable.

Live firing adds something extra to being in the field, namely the danger factor. I was tasked with carrying the grenade launcher too, which was the highlight for me. This one was only firing paint, unfortunately, but it still gave me a rush when I fired it. Whenever you live fire, there is always safety to think about and there is a whole team of soldiers whose job it is to ensure we're safe with firing.

On the first day we went to a range with a few target bunkers and a house roughly five hundred metres apart. It doesn't sound far but when the sun is out in the heat of the Canadian summer and you're carrying your rifle, webbing and a daysack full of ammo, it truly is a lick out. The first day went well with no hiccups and I got best grenade launch of the day, which is the only reason I'm describing the first day!

The next few days were very similar and my confidence was growing with every bunker stormed. I was starting to really enjoy myself and morale was high. In my Warrior, there were six of us: Sergeant James Rose the vehicle commander, Rex the gunner, Steve Castle the mad driver, plus me, Rae and Inglis the crazy piper as the three dismounts in the back of the vehicle. You don't really get to know people until you are in the field with them. James always seemed like a grump to me and I wasn't sure if we were going to get along, but actually I found him to be a good laugh. Inglis was just crazy, talking more shite than I normally do, but he helped keep morale high nonetheless. Rae could be a laugh but I felt he was impeded a little being a dismount commander for the first time. Understandable really, given he was only 19; there was a lot of pressure on this young man's shoulders. A good bunch of guys and it made things so much easier.

As the days passed it was pretty much the same thing day in, day out, occasionally putting fires out as well as we travelled between areas. On one day we were going to be firing that night so we finished earlier than usual. Enough time to have a wash and change my socks, and get a snooze for an hour or two. As darkness fell the skies lit up like fireworks. We also had Challengers with us and when they put the artillery down you couldn't help but jump out of your skin – the Challenger is an awesome machine that puts the Warrior to shame.

We set off to the beginning of the range. As it was a dismounted range we had to walk a few kilometres to the start. Each man had to wear a blue cyalume on the back of his helmet so that the safety knew where you were. It was our turn to go through the range and as we set off the adrenaline slowly increased along with the tension. I was the last man in my platoon, which meant I had a good view of where everybody was. We got orders to move forward and for all the lights to stop so we could travel in darkness – obviously so the enemy couldn't see us. However, that also meant we couldn't see where we were going either.

I had a couple of stumbles, almost going over on my face, but I managed to keep my footing. The last thing you want to do is fall over at night with around 20 kilos of ammo in your webbing on a live fire range, just as you are about two minutes away from an assaulting position. Well, folks, that's exactly what I did! My right foot went straight into a badger hole and it sounded like a snapping twig. I fell to the ground, yelling like a little girl. I knew I had done some damage and wouldn't be able to walk so I lay there yelling until my sergeant (James Rose) came over. At this point I was punching the ground with all my might to distract me from the pain in my foot. He told me to get a grip and shut up, as I'd only probably sprained it. I did shut up, but continued to punch the ground a little longer. The safety staff came over to see what was going on and asked me to straighten my leg then attempt to stand up.

'Stand up! Bloody stand up!'

'Yeah, no problem, Sir. I'll pick myself up then go assault that bunker, why don't I?'

I was in agony but the pain faded slightly, probably due to adrenaline. I took my webbing off then, with a little help, stood on my feet. I tried putting a little weight on my right foot then there was a little, sharp, shooting pain. I'd fractured my foot. The only reason I knew this was because I'd done it a few years earlier and the pain was exactly the same.

Safety went on the radio and got someone to come get me. Future and Mason were the two tasked with getting me to safety. I put an arm around each of their shoulders and hopped like a kangaroo for hundred metres or so until we reached a house. There was a Warrior on its way to pick me up. As I was sitting down, still visibly shaking, the pain came back but ten times worse. I wanted to go to the hospital but I found out that was going to be several hours. I was in the middle of nowhere and there was no quick fix.

All I kept hearing was, 'He sprained his ankle. Sprained!' I've sprained my ankle loads of times and if I could have just stood up I would have chased them away. Eventually I heard the distant sound of a Warrior in the distance and I knew it wouldn't be long. The company sergeant major turned up to evacuate me and I was hoping we would be going to the hospital or at least a medical centre. We drove for half an hour and to my shock ended up back at the camp where we'd started, in the middle of nowhere! While I was in the back of the Warrior lying on the floor with Henderson holding my leg up, I thought it wouldn't be long till I was seeing a doctor. But in the early hours of that morning I had to get my head down on the back of Mr Thom's (PC) Warrior as we were moving first thing. I gratefully took the painkillers and tried my best to sleep.

When we arrived at the main battle group I was told I was going to see the doctor. With the medic on one side and Mr Thom on the other, I hopped over to see them. I'm quite a short man so trying to put my arm around Mr Thom's shoulders was no easy task. If the medic had been a similar size to Mr Thom, they could have picked me up. There was going to be no king's chair for me and I was going to have to hop. I could feel everyone looking at me and I knew they were jealous because I was getting off the exercise with a sprained ankle. A couple of the guys even came over and said 'I fell over too and I'm just getting on with it', and 'I've got a really sore knee'. Yeah, nice one, guys – cheers for that. I don't have the minerals to bluff an injury or make out it's worse than it is. I knew I'd snapped a bone because I'd heard it, so I just did my best not to rise to it.

Finally, a doctor. Now I could relax a little knowing I'd be taken care off. I took my boots off and I already knew what he was going to tell me – I needed an X-ray. An hour later the ambulance came and I went for the X-ray. A few hours after that, the doctor arrived with a cast, which resembled something like Robocop would wear.

'You've fractured your ankle. Come back in two weeks for another X-ray to see how it's healing.'

Yeah, cheers Doc, and off I went. I almost forgot I'd injured myself most of that week until I knocked or twisted it, which brought me back with a bump. It was going to take months until I'd fully recover.

Chapter 23

After being on ceremonial duties in London for nine months, I was sent to the battalion in Catterick. I was scared about going to Afghanistan and that's the reason I had asked to stay in London for longer. I was hopeful my fear would pass, but it took a long time. I was visited by my friends once I arrived in Catterick and they soon changed my mind about being scared. These guys would watch my back as I would theirs. Fear keeps you alive, they said, so I didn't worry about feeling scared.

I stopped drinking, although I did enjoy a whisky from time to time. The problem is, you go out drinking with all ranks and have a laugh, but it's difficult to switch off from that when you're still under the influence. I challenged a sergeant to a fight in front of everyone; he was my friend and I knew he would find it funny but I had forgotten where I was. He yelled at me to get into the office, where I apologised before he got a chance to go at me. He knew I'd been joking, but he had to show it wasn't tolerated. I understood that, of course. and luckily drinking was rare in the battalion.

I had been off duty for the weekend so I spent it in Edinburgh. I didn't have to be back at the barracks until lunchtime on the Monday so that meant getting an extra night at home. December 5th was an ordinary day. I woke up early to get a bus down to the Borders where my good friend Hawthorn would pick me up and take me the rest of the way to Catterick. It was snowing very heavily and the hills looked beautiful. As the bus pulled up the snow stopped and blinding sun came out. That's Scotland for you, never a dull moment.

I jumped in the front of Hawthorn's car and Travis jumped in the back. We set off and discussed the highlight of our weekends, namely how much we drank in true Scottish fashion. I still felt rough from the litre of whisky I'd had on Saturday and soon it went quiet. It was cosy with the heaters on and the warmth of the sun. Nobody spoke and I was soon dozing off.

'Oh shit, oh shit!' Hawthorn yelped.

I opened my eyes and realised the car was going into a skid.

'Turn left!' I shouted.

Hawthorn was travelling at 60mph and although we managed to steer into the skid the car was always going to be leaving the road. As we snaked to and fro it was only a matter of time before we hit the field. Unfortunately, as we left the road we hit a massive boulder on my side and the impact threw me to the roof. As I came back down, I knew I had hurt my back.

The car was still travelling at speed and I thought my time was up. We jumped over the boulder and hit a massive ditch that was approximately fifty metres from top to bottom. Hawthorn was still shouting, 'Oh shit, oh shit', and I realised that it wasn't over. We hit long grass and a mound of dirt that threw me against the dashboard. I smashed my face against it and saw the blood travelling horizontally towards the dash as I flew back into my seat. My face was a mess, but the pain was nothing compared to the intense pain in my lower back.

The car finally stopped and to add insult to injury the flaming airbag had the cheek to go off.

Travis shouted: 'Boggie, get out!'

It was over. Apart from the engine bay beginning to smoke, we were out of danger. The smell of smoke increased and we could also smell burning rubber. It was a two-door car and I would have to move to allow Travis to get out. I never checked on Hawthorn, but he managed to get out swiftly. But at the time I didn't know this so I would have to move. I clicked my belt off and opened the door. The long grass came into the car as I moved my left leg out, shortly followed by the right. I tried to stand up but to my horror I collapsed onto the grass. At least now Travis would be able to get away from the smoking car.

I on the other hand wouldn't have it so easy. I knew I was in danger and needed to get away. I grabbed a bunch of the long grass and pulled myself bunch after bunch away as far as possible. I got about fifteen metres away then almost passed out with the pain in my lower back. I tried to move into a position that took the pain away, but there wasn't one. I decided to pull my clothes up my back and lower myself into the snow in the hope it would numb the pain. It didn't. All it did was make me very cold and I began to shiver uncontrollably. Both my friends were up and walking about a little dazed, but they seemed okay.

The paramedics arrived thirty or forty minutes later and struggled to get to me. A lovely Asian woman had stopped and held my hand for a while and kept me awake until the ambulance got to me. My friends tried to encourage me to move, but I snapped at them to leave me alone. The pain was unbearable. Even after the paramedics gave me a 10ml jab of morphine jab I was begging for more. They told me I could only have 10ml while in transit, so I had a horrible time in the ambulance. Once I arrived at the hospital in Newcastle I was taken into a room and a nurse arrived with morphine. She began adding 5ml jabs until I couldn't feel the pain anymore. It took four jabs.

I had to go on a different back board to go for an MRI scan. I screamed as they slid me over and almost cried. The scan confirmed I had broken my back and also that my L1 vertebra was thirty per cent crushed.

The following night I was put into a ward with mixed patients. There were two old boys in their 70s and some young laddies who had also been in a road traffic accident.

The nurses came to my bedside and said they were taking me to the theatre. I freaked out at them as I thought they meant to a pantomime, it being December after all. Once I realised they wanted to operate I asked if that was my only option. The specialist arrived the following night and asked why I had refused surgery. It had a seventy per cent success rate and my dad had had problems after a back operation. I asked the specialist for an alternative. He told me my spine was very unstable and I would have to lie without moving for three weeks minimum. If he operated I could be on my feet after a couple of days. I decided not to risk it as the specialist wouldn't guarantee I would be able to walk after it.

I was a heavy smoker back then so my coughing was causing the worst sharp pain, closely followed by sneezing. I threatened to discharge myself after three days as I was no longer allowed morphine and had been put on ibuprofen and codeine. The doctors doubled my dose, but it still wasn't enough. I rang my buzzer so many times and was mostly ignored. They told me I could only have medication every four hours. As a former heroin addict, it must have affected my tolerance.

After three weeks from hell I got word I was to be transported. My back brace arrived and I was finally allowed to go back to Edinburgh. I pleaded with the ambulance driver to pull over at Berwick so I could have my first cigarette in three weeks. I got a massive head rush and felt dizzy. My week in the Edinburgh Royal Infirmary was much more pleasant. I had tons more visitors and I was allowed a cigarette. In hospital I had a wheelchair and the nurses were happy for me to be wheeled out for a cigarette. My dad works for the Scottish ambulance service and was always in to see me most mornings. Newspapers, juice and, of course, some tobacco to keep me going.

One night late on a guy over from me had a visitor. I was lying watching DVDs on my laptop when shortly after I heard the curtains being drawn and whispering, then the unmistakable noise of the foil. They were having a smoke of heroin.

I needed to go home. Finally a physio came round and asked me to climb six stairs up and then down. I managed it no problem so she was happy to discharge me. Whoop, whoop, I'm going home to my own bed! My friend Lisa had visited me often and she agreed to take me to my mum's first, although my mum freaked at me until she realised Lisa had brought me and I hadn't just discharged myself.

I could finally get some peace. No more screaming patients, no more heroin users – it was bliss. My friend Ben had been looking after the flat for me and bent over backwards to accommodate me. I couldn't move very easily so relied on the kindness of others.

My appetite wasn't there and I had dropped back to nine stone. I would sit on my bed listening to Rod Stewart, Wet Wet Wet and Take That trying to focus on recovery, but the drugs were taking over and all I wanted was morphine. Every time I sneezed, morphine. Every time I coughed, morphine. Getting up from the sofa, morphine. A doctor wouldn't prescribe me any so I started thinking if I could buy any on the streets. That felt horrible but I felt it was necessary at the time.

Back in my Safeway days, I had met a girl called Stephanie. We'd had a wee thing years before but I was on heroin so it never went anywhere. I had fancied her for ages and I remember she grabbed my belt buckle in the bus stop, but I had a bag of heroin in the house so I quickly made my excuses and left.

Steph had been messaging me while I was in hospital in Edinburgh and we arranged for her to visit me at my flat. We had always had a laugh and that's what I needed. I had four weeks' of hair growth that was needing shaved off and Steph kindly shaved me. She took some pics of the different stages: I looked like Zangief from Street Fighter at first, then Cyrus the Virus from Con Air, then finally the druggie I had looked like for most of my life.

Steph had no experience with illegal drugs so found it difficult to advise me. 'If you're in pain, you need to do something,' she would say. My pill popping was getting out of control and I felt like a zombie again. I had given up cannabis years prior to joining the army, but if it

74

helped I'd go back to smoking hash. So I started smoking again, but I was on too many tablets and soon got melted. Lying in bed semi-conscious wasn't what I wanted, but at least the physical pain had eased. Cannabis does have negative side effects for someone like me: paranoid, paranoid, paranoid. I wouldn't go out, nor did I want to speak to or see anyone. They would pity me, or worry I would end up back on heroin. I understand why and although I think about heroin every day I know I would never use it again.

Steph and I were getting really close, but I'd decided nobody could or would put up with me. However, as time passed, I realised that she was making me happy and I decided not to push her away like I had done in previous relationships.

My issues with addiction and mental health would have been a lot worse if I had been on my own. Fortunately, I managed not to drive Steph away although we did have our moments. Cherise, Steph's eight-year-old daughter, was adorable, but I could see she was spoilt and her mum didn't seem to mind. I was always going to be strict as I believe it's the best way of teaching kids who otherwise won't listen. Cherise didn't like me shouting and thankfully I only had to raise my voice a handful of times. We were a perfect little family and that kept me focused on recovery.

Chapter 24

After my car crash, I returned to Catterick and remember all too well the day the battalion returned from Afghanistan. I hid in the corner of the scoff house and never held eye contact with my friends. That was one of the hardest things I have ever done. A close second was being put in charge of dealing with all their medals. All the things you would perhaps think were the hardest were easy for me. Not taking part destroyed me inside. I was so proud of everyone but I couldn't bring myself to look or talk to them. I did make a nice cuppa but I couldn't do that forever.

Everyone knew I wasn't bluffing with my injuries from the crash, so I got help from all ranks. I always liked the officers in the army because they were from a different world from me. Most knew of my drug past and we often spoke about it at length.

I attended three rehab courses while in the army along with hydrotherapy, acupuncture and some other courses. I was broken physically and my mind was breaking, too. If I couldn't soldier on then I had to think about my future. Becoming a drugs counsellor was always my Plan B for after the army, but that didn't quite work out. My own addiction would see to that. Medical discharge was my only option.

Not being able to put my training into practice has always haunted me. I felt like a failure even though I hadn't done anything wrong. I try not to dwell on it but it's difficult if you're not being proactive. Occupying my mind with anything else worked, but I had to be careful to only put positive thoughts in there. Focusing on my own drug problems wouldn't help, as I later found out.

If I had to sum up my time in the army, I would say close but no cigar. That may sound strange as I was a Scots Guardsman for five years. Joining at 30 made it unique enough, but from where I'd come I didn't think I'd get past basic training. Pre-deployment for Afghanistan had started and I came so close to being a hero. I'll never know what would have happened to me over there, I wasn't going for any other reason than to look after my newfound brothers. They proved time and time again that they had my back and I showed them I had theirs. It's what we are taught.

After my accident I was put on tramadol and it really affected my mental health. I was lucky to be alive, so I tried to always remember that. But as time passed I felt I was slipping back into a life of drug addiction, only this time I needed them for the physical pain in my back.

I went to the military doctor to ask if there was anything else I could try as tramadol is an opiate. The doctor fully understood and we began trials for an alternative. Pregabalin was the first drug I tried; I didn't feel any withdrawal when I switched because I did it gradually. After two weeks on pregabalin I noticed I was starting to think about suicide. I would cry for no apparent reason and it really scared me. Luckily, I was in a place to be able to notice the signs of depression, so I went straight back to the doctor. It was clear pregabalin was not for me so co-codamol was next. The problem was my past addictions. I discussed it with the doctor at length and we decided to stick to tablets I knew. I was still serving in the army but my health limited the jobs I could do.

Finally, after intensive rehabilitation courses and the realisation I wasn't going to be able to soldier on, I took the advice of the doctors and physios and took the medical discharge. I hated that because I was leaving a job that wasn't just a job, it was a whole new life I'd created and I loved it. I could see and hear the pity from friends and even people who I didn't know too well.

I headed back to Edinburgh for the last time. It was a hard three-hour drive from Catterick. I was an addict back on opiates and as soon as I took my uniform off for the last time I felt sad and angry.

I'd beaten heroin so surely prescribed drugs would be a canter. I kept telling myself it wasn't my fault, but the feeling of the opiates had started to take over again. I slipped back into talking to myself negatively without realising and that affected my ability to stay positive. I think if I'd been left on my own, my mood would have thrown me back to my heroin lifestyle. My happiness would be dictated by the tablets and that was a bitter pill to swallow. I needed to get away from opiates or I would destroy my life. I couldn't stay on drugs that cloud my judgement like opiates. The feeling of not caring is easy at the time, but it affects your mind. Everyone has a heart, but not everyone knows how to use it.

Although I knew I would never take heroin again there are other drugs that feel similar that you can get from the doctor. Drugs are readily available and it can be easy to fall into that trap. The reason drugs of all kinds are so popular is that they feel great. Heroin, cocaine, crack, pills, cannabis – all have pros and cons and weighing up risk when you're unhappy is difficult. These man-made drugs can properly destroy your insides too. I was on twenty-three tablets from the doctor at one point – twenty-three! I felt like a zombie every day and I didn't care. My back was agony so I did not question what I was doing until later.

I'm delighted to announce that I've cut my daily intake to just four co-codamol 30/500s per day. I used grass to help me, and I have no problem sharing that with the world.

I plan to change the law on cannabis in this country and to educate – I'm not the most literate person in the world, but I have a gift of knowledge. A way to save lives. A way to bring change to our suffering people. If this makes no sense to you then that's ok, I am writing this book for the people who can be saved. I will train these people myself if need be to become the best counsellors. Who better to sit and talk with about your situation than someone who has been there and knows a way out? It won't be for everyone but if it helps just one person then it's a great cause.

I have smoked solid cannabis for most of my life. In the early years it was to fit in, but more recently it helps my back pain. I ran out of solid and then I could only get grass. I find it strong, so I put only a little bit in a one-skinner. Everything changed that night and I want to share it with the world because it guided me to my next chapter. It's been a crazy rollercoaster, but all positive. I can help people and I never thought it was possible. The army taught me so much about myself as did my drug addictions. I will help anyone who is struggling. I've tried most drugs and I understand why you will end up addicted to them.

However, there are people out there right now who see no way out. The reason they feel this way is because they are not in control of their own minds. The problem is they have given up. When I teach these people how to help themselves things will make sense. It won't be easy, but if it's now possible because of my story then it's a good job done by me.

Chapter 25

Straight after leaving the army, Help for Heroes offered me the opportunity to do a three-month course for Princes Trust, working with young people who were struggling with problems at school or at home. I loved working with the youngsters – they all had so much potential. Drugs were an issue for some of them and I was told not to discuss anything like that with them. I didn't understand or agree with that decision. If you only have people who have lived perfect sheltered lives, then they won't relate to these young people. I could have helped much more, but I was often overlooked. I offered to do military exercises when we went away for a week to do teamwork exercises, but I was chinned off and thought I was wasting my time there. It's a great idea to do these programmes but you need to have a mixture of different backgrounds to have a better chance of helping,

I left the course feeling a bit underwhelmed and decided to try and get my peer support badge. I enjoyed that course because everyone was interested in my experience and knowledge of certain things. I passed my exam and was now a qualified peer support worker. My first client was having issues with heroin, but I made excuses not to go. My reason was that I felt like a hypocrite. I was struggling with my own opiate addiction and didn't feel in the right frame of mind. I didn't take that well, but I learned a massive amount on that course.

I still needed to do something so I decided to get my SIA badge, which would qualify me for security work. The course was common sense for the most part. Again I passed and I went for an interview at Scottish Widows, of all places. My memories of smoking heroin in the toilets there came to mind, but I was better now and could prove it. However, I didn't get the job because of my back problems. Offers of jobs came in, but working on the doors didn't appeal to me. I had completed another course, but nothing seemed to fit.

I will be my own boss, I decided. No more being shouted at sounds good, I'll do the shouting from now on, I thought. I invested in some equipment to start a new business. I bought an industrial powder coating oven that holds twelve alloys at once, flocking kits, carbon fibre twill and all the resins to go with it. I bought a whole hydro-dipping business from a man in Ayr who was selling up. However, the deal collapsed. I've always jumped in first and in most cases I have been left thinking, why did I do that. Lesson learned, or so I thought. I invested in another business and was bumped out of £5,000. That was the final straw for me. I am too trusting and I can't help that, unfortunately. I wished I could see these folk for what they were before I'd handed over my money. I have learned that I need guidance in business and that's what I'm doing now – I have people that I trust looking over everything I do now. If people want my money then I will show them the door.

Since leaving the army I was still struggling with drug addiction. I was trapped in my flat, which held bad memories, so I really needed to get away from Edinburgh. I moved to Fife to try and better myself and stop taking so many tablets, but my addiction followed me and I began turning into a zombie again. Talking to myself kept me sane but I knew something wasn't right. What was I doing with my life? I tried different things but I always ended up back on drugs, prescribed or not. If I took enough of my tablets I could get stoned like I was on heroin almost. It was a horrible feeling and it was destroying me physically and mentally. I didn't go through all that crap to end up a druggie again.

Thankfully I realised what was going on. I was worrying about my daughter and my feelings of guilt for leaving her weighed heavy on my heart and mind. I started to think how I could make her proud of me. Everything aligned for once and I found myself with more answers than questions.

I thought about how I could help others and immediately thought of becoming a drug counsellor, but if I was capable of doing more then I would.

I'm financially stable so I don't need to work for anyone and I'm in a great position to make some big changes on my own. I plan to do it alone but the more support I can get the quicker the problems will get fixed. My plans sound ambitious to everyone, no doubt, but if the only thing standing in the way is money then I will source it. Money makes the world go round, no matter where you are, I have never respected money since my heroin addiction ended. I hate how it makes people evil and full of greed and jealousy. The world doesn't owe these people anything but they think it does and will try to steal to benefit themselves financially. Their guilt will eventually catch up with them.

I'm at peace now and long may it continue, as I am now officially less of a wanker. Everybody has a wanker in them – people will try to deny that but these same people have never made any mistakes and think they are perfect, Beauty is internal and will always shine outwards. We use our eyes to judge, but our voices and ears to learn about people. I judge a book by its cover initially; it's difficult not to, it's how we work as humans. However, if you

80

realise you're doing it you can go out of your way to prove you were wrong to judge. It doesn't work all the time, but more times than not you will be proven wrong.

Please understand that most addicts will have their guard up. You can only build trust by taking time to break down barriers. Once you have trust they will open up and then you have a chance to really get to the root of their problems. Some things can't be fixed but training your mind will mean you can forget a lot of stuff that's pulling you down. Take baby steps if need be or one big swoop like how I did it. All that matters is we work towards a better life.

Sometimes when I'm daydreaming I wonder what it would be like to receive mail from addicts saying that they read my book or saw a social media video and it worked, that they stopped like I did. I don't think I'm special enough that I'm the only person it can happen to, which is why I'm writing about it. You need to believe it really happened. If you can do that then you are set to make a better life much more quickly. If not, keep chipping away until one day, BANG it happens, and you won't be able to contain yourself. Life goes on as normal for everyone else but you have changed instantly forever.

I have strayed off my path since but I catch myself every time. You can do the same. No more of my life will I be thinking of death. Reaching 40 was tough as I wasn't doing anything productive with my time. I felt lost as I'd been waiting for this switch in my head to go off for years. I knew it was there but didn't know where – it turned out it was my memories. I was thinking about not seeing my daughter, reaching 40, health issues and a lack of motivation. I made a deal with myself that night to make my daughter proud.

Chapter 26

I never thought I'd get married, I always saw myself consumed by drugs, and women were not part of my life. There were very few women I would have considered settling down with and, as it turned out, nobody made me happy. That changed when I met my wife, Stephanie. I wouldn't be the man I am today without her. I'm hard work for anyone, but Steph knew how to take me. When I needed to vent she would listen and, most importantly, didn't judge me for using drugs. That wouldn't have worked, but thankfully it was never a problem. I don't drink and don't take Valium as these are drugs that I know she doesn't like me on. She is ok with painkillers because they ease my back pain. I hid my addiction problems for years as I thought I'd snap out of it. That took longer than expected but it did happen.

We did discuss my use of cannabis. I didn't want anyone to think I was going to end up back on heroin, as in some people's eyes that's how it all begins. For me it was for medicinal purposes as it would allow me to reduce my tablets. It worked for a while but then I'd put my back out and be laid up for a month. I could reduce my tablets over a few weeks or months, but all was lost when the pain was severe. I needed morphine one time, but ended up on twenty-three tablets a day – it's a vicious cycle. Without the pain in my back I don't think I'd take any drugs. Smoking tobacco will be my hardest addiction to overcome, but I think I can stop that too. I'm not looking for surgery at the moment, so I will battle on.

We went to Caesar's Palace to get married, which I never thought would be possible. I'd dreamed of Las Vegas from all the films I'd seen. Getting married was the best day of my life – I had a best pal who I loved.

I couldn't believe my luck when I met Steph the second time round after my accident. I'd fancied her since my Safeway days and we hit it off straight away. I am cheeky as hell and most girls struggled with my humour, but Steph gives it back. We always end up belly laughing at how cheeky we are with each other. Behind every good man is a good woman, they say, and that's certainly true of my life now. Loneliness isn't very nice. Even in previous relationships I'd been lonely. Steph knows everything about me and it's refreshing to feel comfortable enough to talk about things that I do. I've always known Steph's thoughts about my life, and even my struggle with addiction in recent times has been made easier with her support.

I always said I would never marry, but I knew Steph wanted to get married. I had a choice to make. I got married because I wanted to be with Steph and if marriage was part of the deal then I was in. It's just a bit of paper to me that means nothing. What I feel in my heart is my bit of paper.

I hate flying now so getting to Vegas was difficult. I was a nervous wreck the whole flight. The doctor prescribed me 10mg of Valium, which wore off quickly. I used to swallow 160mg in one go so it's no wonder. My back played up – it seized up a lot and the turbulence didn't help. The plane's engines made a whining noise, like in the Tom Hanks film Castaway, but people continued to eat their scoff. I gripped my seat and braced right up preparing for impact, to the amusement of the other passengers. But when we landed it was special. A limo was waiting to take us to the Luxor, where we would stay for most of the time.

We are all gamblers in our family, but Steph's family don't so we often split up to get a fix. Slots were everyone's favourites. Only fools play slots – it takes no skill whatsoever. If you're going to gamble play cards or gamble on a calculated risk. I'm not saying gambling is right, especially when you can't afford it, but you have to use your brain to work out the best chance of winning. Although gambling isn't Steph's thing, she picks horses for me and wins on the Grand National all the time. Luckily for me, Steph loves to shop, so it worked out great. Her dad was looking after the bairn for us so we could be romantic, holding hands and kissing all the time like a couple of teenagers.

I felt sad on our first day as I'd wanted to get married in uniform, ideally with a medal on my chest, but I couldn't let it affect my time in Vegas. The kilt is just as good and I wore Help for Heroes tartan, so I still felt proud of my army days.

I didn't feel at all nervous when the big day arrived – until I saw Steph come out with her dad. My heart stopped for a split second then I welled up. I was so in love that it took over the feeling of loneliness in my life. Soulmates forever and that's special. We rarely argue seriously, just petty 'it's your turn to make the cuppa' type. Steph loves her own jokes and I often laugh at her laughing as opposed to the crap joke she just told. We constantly take the piss out of each other and I love it. It just works perfectly and I'm a lucky man for sure.

We went for food after and I gave a speech. Yes, I cried. I am an emotional man. We headed up the Eiffel Tower for a look along The Strip and we were congratulated everywhere we went. Everyone was smiling at us. I thought it was great because I usually have a frown on my face and it's a defence thing. I want to look unapproachable sometimes as I attract the bampots. Not bad people, but crazy people. I always said it's best to get on with the crazy people as you're better being a friend than a foe. It's worked well for me. I don't always agree with what people do, but I try to understand. I have always shown respect first. Some people are the opposite and wait on it. I don't want to not know these people so I always try to break the ice, hold doors open, say hello, wave at strangers. My anger issues mean I can fly off the handle when I respect someone, only for them to disrespect me. I am getting better at not losing my shit. It's a challenge but I'm trying my hardest. I'm quick to apologise too, even if I'm not in the wrong; the reason is not cowardliness but giving myself a talking to. I can switch it on a moment's notice now, but I'll always lose my shit at times because I'm passionate.

We stayed in Caesar's Palace on our wedding night. I lit a cigar in the hot tub with a glass of champagne just so I could say to Steph: 'Say hello to my little friend.' Room service delivered an incredible breakfast as we sat looking out over Vegas. I didn't want to come home and the flight was preying on my mind too.

On the last day I played Three Card Brag, a game I thought I knew. It was our last card game before we had to leave. I put thirty dollars down and said to the dealer: 'All in.' She gave me a funny look and tried to explain the rules, but I didn't listen. My wee brother was hurrying me up, so I just wanted a bet. She dealt me a 3 and an 8 of diamonds. I said, 'all in', and again she looked bewildered. 'You sure?' I said yes, my wee bro said no and the dealer looked too and advised me again of the rules. She flipped over three more cards: 2, 5 and 7 of diamonds. She freaked out and shouted for the pit boss.

I looked at my bro and said: 'Did I win?'

'Aye, you idiot,' was his reply.

I started celebrating. The pit boss said, Congratulations, Sir' and I got my $300. If I'd hit the 4 of diamonds instead of the 2 or 8, I would have got $4,000. Bitter sweet, but a great memory.

Flying time again. Next time I go long haul I'm getting a cabin with a bed and a box of Valium or I'm not going.

84

Steph's daughter Cherise was eight when me and her mum got together. She was an adorable little bairn who knew how to get what she wanted, she had Mummy wrapped around her finger. But she was well behaved and had manners too, so it was easy bringing her up to be the young woman she is today. We have had our moments of course, but not many – there was the time she nearly burned the house down after leaving the gas on, and the time she cut slices of cheese then placed them on bread and put them in the toaster. But that was the worst of it. Cherise was a well-behaved bairn.

I wouldn't go on holiday abroad if I didn't have Steph and Cherise to think about. I enjoy it when I'm there, of course, but it's not fair to deprive them of my silliness. We went on a cruise for my 40th and I preferred it. Would the ship sink though? That was constantly on my mind. It won't be my last cruise, that's for sure. It wasn't a yacht I was on, this thing had shops, gyms, restaurants and swimming pools, and the entertainment was amazing. I'd recommend everyone to try it once. The flights were short too, so not too bad.

Chapter 27

Mine and Steph's first holiday abroad was in Lanzarote in February 2015. It was just the two of us as Cherise was away to Lagginlea with the school for the week. Steph's niece was going to house-sit and then watch Cherise for a couple of days till we got back.

Five hours on a plane was hard work. I can clearly remember gripping Steph's arm hard. I thought we were going to crash-land, the way the plane was turning as we hit the runway. Safe to say after that a stiff drink was needed. The hotel was really nice and quiet and it was so good to just be the two of us. For the whole week we literally lazed about, had nice meals and were in bed by 11 most nights, playing cards. Rock 'n' roll! But we had the best time.

That's when we decided we would get married in Las Vegas the following year. Steph didn't want a big wedding and we both thought why not, so it was decided. Viva Las Vegas, baby! Lanzarote was one of our best holidays, it probably helped that we only had each other to please and did everything at our own leisure.

Since we got married, we have gone on a big family holiday every year to Turkey. There are usually about ten of us, sometimes more. I love it. We always have a great time and it is nice to spend it with my family. For our first holiday after we got married we went to Hisarönü. As soon as we arrived, we knew it was going to be great. We went straight to the bar even though none of us are really drinkers – other than Kyle. And we pretty much claimed the pool table as ours – even the bairn was getting a game.

Daytimes were spent by the pool, with everyone usually watching Kyle trying to drown the bairn, or vice versa, but it was all good fun. At night everyone would get dressed up and we would go for a nice big family meal. Afterwards the women would nose around the shops, which usually left me out of pocket for some bags or earrings Steph or the bairn had to have. Then it would be back to the hotel where we would play pool – usually me and my dad against Kyle and Steph's dad, while the women sat having a blether and topping up the bar bill, even if it was just coffees.

Kyle had to leave earlier than the rest of us as it was his and his wife's first wedding anniversary. The night before he left, we all went out for our last meal altogether and afterwards we ended up having a shot at virtual reality masks in the middle of the street. I don't think any of us have laughed as hard as that for a long time. When you had the mask on it was like you were on a rollercoaster. The screaming by everyone who tried it was great to watch, including when I had my turn, no doubt. The track disappeared and you're left freefalling. We walked back to the apartment rather than taking our usual taxi back as Lisa had been skydiving earlier on in the holiday and had to go pick up the video from it. Steph went with her.

At the place we agreed to meet up, we found this wee arcade with shooting and crazy golf. It was one of those nights you didn't plan, but ended up being one to remember. Kyle had another go on the virtual reality in there and the guy running it was tickling his leg with sticks. Kyle's screams were unreal, we were all in fits of laughter again. We were in the middle of crazy golf by the time Steph and Lisa came back. They sat on big bean bags having a juice and a blether, until the bairn decided she wanted to go on the trampoline. They couldn't just let her go, oh no! Steph, Lisa and Lisa's daughter had to have a shot as well. I videoed them all. Cherise was just a wee thing so was bouncing from her bum to knees no problem. Then there was my wife, who happened to have a dress on by the way; it's fair to say she wasn't a natural, although she gave it a good go. I I don't think we all laughed as hard as that in a long time.

In 2019 I turned 40. I'd been dreading it for a long time, so we decided that we would go on a cruise for my birthday. Me, Steph and my mum and my dad booked a week on the Marella Dream. We left just before my birthday and set sail from Palma, from where we sailed to Livorno, Savona, Monaco, Toulon, Barcelona and then back to Palma. It was an amazing experience and other than one night when it was a bit rough at sea, you literally forgot you were on a boat half the time. We made the most of the sightseeing every day, going to the Leaning Tower of Pisa and the Casino de Monte Carlo. Every night we got dressed to go for a nice meal where everyone couldn't do enough for you. After our meal we would watch the evening show – it was like going to the theatre every night, the shows were so good.

I won't forget my 40th birthday in a hurry. My wife had booked us into a restaurant on the top deck, where you cooked your steak on a hot stone in front of yourself. I'd never experienced anything like it. After our three-course meal they brought out a cake Steph had arranged and everyone in the restaurant sang Happy Birthday to me. Maybe being 40 wasn't so bad after all. We had loads to look forward to once we got home seeing our pup again and then moving to our forever home just a couple of weeks later.

We love going to Turkey. More family members have come along each time and I'll never forget all the memories we have made together. In the last couple of years even my Uncle Duncan has come along; he usually spends his days shopping for watches and t-shirts. The last three years we have stayed at Icmeler. Mum and Dad had been going there for years and had met a man called Captain Eric who has his own boat and did private boat trips every day from Marmaris. That has always been a highlight for us – sailing around the Med, with just family on the boat catching the sun and then stopping off and cooling down in the sea, with the usual show-offs jumping into the water.

The first holiday I, Steph and Cherise went on with my family was in 2013. Cherise couldn't swim so I spent the holiday trying to teach her only for her to chin me off and listen to Uncle Kyle. He took all the glory for teaching her and now I was watching her jumping off the boat into the ocean. It's great being in the ocean till you look down and can't see anything and you swear something has touched your foot, so you swim for your life back to the boat because you swear a shark is lurking down there. Captain Eric made the best spaghetti and chicken for lunch. His wife would even send him with extra dishes for us all. We were usually all stuffed and ready for a sleep after lunch, so I would head to the top of the boat, put my headphones on and relax in the sun only for Steph to start spraying me with more sun protection so I didn't burn.

As soon as Eric stopped at Icmeler on the way back and we all got off the boat, you realised how tiring it is being at sea. We would drag ourselves back to the hotel for a good forty winks.

Turkey has always been our go-to destination as a family; I'm sure I'll be back again but there is more to see in this world – travel broadens the mind. I had an offer to go scuba diving in Egypt, but I'm afraid of sharks. Basically, my shadow would give me a fright when I'm underwater. I'm totally fascinated by all wildlife, but the ocean-goers are awesome. The orca is my favourite, although the flipper comes a close second. It started with Free Willy, but I've educated myself a bit over the years. They are so intelligent.

The last day of the holiday is always bitter sweet. You don't want the holiday to be over, but at the same time you just want to be home. This was especially true for our last holiday as Steph and me had missed our dog Caesar so much plus we had only recently moved house so we were looking forward to getting home even more.

The flight was always the worst part for me. I am usually really quiet the whole day just waiting to board. Steph doesn't mind too much as she is usually busy in Duty Free. This is the first year (2020) that we haven't planned a holiday. We decided to spend the time in our new house and do bits to the garden. Probably the real reason is Steph doesn't want to leave Caesar again or she would have been dropping hints about going every chance she got. The new house is like being on holiday constantly.

Chapter 28

The newest addition to our family our Rottweiler, Caesar. Steph and the bairn had gone on for years about getting a dog. We had a hamster called Harry who was mental. He would swing from his cage and could easily get out of the exercise ball, so we had to sellotape him in. When Harry passed away we got two guinea pigs, Zayn and Ollie. The bairn and Steph didn't like picking them up and because they were in the house we felt bad, so we ended up giving them away.

At the end of October 2018, I finally gave in and told Steph that we could get a dog but it was between a Rottweiler and a German Shepherd, so the bairn could pick. When I told her I never saw smiles like it. Of course, they were straight on their phones googling puppies, before deciding a Rottweiler it was to be.

Steph managed to find some puppies that were for sale just five minutes up the road from us. We arranged a visit and when we got there it was the three of us and another woman. Luckily Steph had contacted the seller first so we had the pick of the litter. We already knew we were getting a boy and there were three to choose from. Steph got the one with the red collar, Cherise the one with the grey collar and I the one with the green collar. Obviously, we all wanted the pup we were holding but I could see right away Steph was smitten. The one she was holding was also the heaviest of the litter. Once I'd a good look at him, I was the same as Steph, who was adamant she wouldn't hold another one. It was just the bairn to convince now, which was easy. The pup started kissing Cherise all over her face and that was it. We had decided red collar it is. He would be known as Caesar.

We all love him. He was eight weeks old when we got him and he was adorable. The only problem was we now had a three-week wait until we could bring him home. Steph and Cherise managed to pass some of the time by shopping for him – spoilt wasn't the word for it. Steph and the bairn went to pick him up after what felt like a six-month wait, while I waited patiently in the house. When I saw them coming up the stairs, I couldn't wait to hold the wee bundle in Steph's arms. He fitted perfectly in my hand and had the softest fur.

I had never had a dog before so I was adamant that he was going to be good and I wouldn't let him get away with anything. I was tough on him from the start as I knew he was going to try to dominate us. I've read dog whisperers' books and knew I had to be pack leader. I would follow him around everywhere making sure he wasn't up to no good and he knew exactly what was going on.

From the moment he came into the house he went to the puppy mats for the toilet until he was allowed out, then he became a bit of a chancer for a bit: one foot on the mat and wee on the carpet. He has been trained to sit and paw and he has never snatched food although he does like to keep at least one eye on you when you're eating just in case there's any leftovers for him. Other than a couple of sock casualties he has not tried to chew anything. As he got older he was trying to control us and that wouldn't fly. I'm strict and so he had to learn to behave. He picked it up without much fuss, never jumping up in the kitchen or going to the toilet indoors. Caesar is too smart for his own good at times. We rarely raise our voices in anger but he follows Steph everywhere.

I felt like I didn't sit down for the first six months we had him, but it was all worth it. Sometimes Steph thought I was too harsh on him, but she also knows that he wouldn't be the dog he is today if I hadn't been. He is still a nightmare when we have family over, as he thinks he is a wee lap dog and not the size he is. Because he gets all of Steph's attention, he thinks everyone else should be the same with him, and usually they do right enough.

When we moved to a bigger house, we had the space to get him a crate so he would sleep in it. And if he was naughty that was where he would go. The first few months after we moved, he was never out of it. He was constantly pushing his boundaries to see how far he could get, but now he has the roam of the house. When we are out he has the whole hall, top and bottom At night-time, as soon as Steph says goodnight to me he is off like a whippet, the wee Judas, to sleep at the bottom of the bed. The two of them snore, but Caesar huffs and puffs so I'll kick him out if he gets too loud. Steph wouldn't take kindly to me trying to kick her out, that's for sure. He hardly leaves her side and she loves it. He's not much of a guard dog, but he was the perfect addition to our wee family. I may take professional training lessons. I think Caesar needs a pal so I'm getting another puppy. I want a pack of at least four Rotties and I'd like to get them pulling a sled.

We are an awesome team and an awesome family. Laughing is an everyday occurrence and it's special to me. Happiness is priceless and we are very happy together. I'm no longer alone in my life and it feels amazing.

My whole family has supported me from the day they realised I was in trouble with drugs. I don't think I'd be here if they hadn't. I often dreamed of making them proud while I was still using, but it was only a dream back then. Dreams don't come true, I thought at the time. Getting clean would be a start and maybe they would be proud if I could achieve that. They were indeed proud once I got clean, but there was something missing. I didn't feel proud. I felt ashamed, as I always will. The only way for me to combat that was to do some good with my time. It was a shock for everyone when I joined the army – including me. I was focused on making a difference and the army would help me. I had already lived my life so I wouldn't be easily broken, mentally or physically. The army taught me much more than I could ever have dreamed. It was a shame I was medically discharged, but then I wouldn't be on this journey. I have to believe everything happens for a reason. I spoke of not getting clean for myself, but for my family and that is true. As time passed, I did feel better about myself but initially it was all about my family.

My family means the world to me and I could not have done any of the things I did without them. I think I'd be clear of heroin though. My feelings of guilt and shame were the reason I joined the army, and then later starting my own charity. My daughter will hopefully be proud of me even though I no longer get to see her. One thing I realised was that I had to focus on getting myself better. The arguments with my daughter's mother were destroying me inside, which was why I decided to leave.

Living in Lochend was like living in a prison. I lived there with my daughter until she was three years old. It was not easy living with those memories every day, the same noises that used to petrify me, the frequent threats to kick my door in. Whether it was people demanding drugs or other reasons, the fear was real and I would sleep with weapons at hand as I reacted to every noise outside. When I joined the army I could finally escape that life.

Five years away from Lochend made me happy, but I was only in the flat for a few days after getting home from hospital and it felt like a prison again. This time I couldn't even walk so I was trapped.

I have seen my daughter a few times in recent years so I know she is ok. I had the opportunity to buy my council flat so I saw that as a way out. I needed somewhere I could get peace – no offers of heroin, no asking me to be a chauffeur, no sleepless nights because the stair door opened. I was waiting for her to get in touch while I was writing this book, so I could finish it but I realised I had mixed it up. If I wanted her to be proud of her dad then sitting playing Xbox all day wouldn't cut it. She would not understand why I had to finish with her mum but in time I hoped I'd get the chance to tell her.

I now live in a lovely area and it's so peaceful. Moving has helped my mental health massively. I prefer animals over humans. I'm surrounded by cows, sheep and other types of wildlife you don't see in cities so much.

The whole family loves it here and I'm so glad. I thought I'd be trapped forever in that flat. I don't worry much because of Caesar – he is an amazing dog and so intelligent, he will protect Steph and the bairn when I'm not there. Cherise will be driving soon too, so her freedom will be restored. I know it was difficult for her to leave her friends and family, but thankfully she loves it too.

I would move back to Edinburgh if they didn't love it but I wouldn't be staying in the flat. Property in the city is so expensive, but we were able to get an actual house with an upstairs, something I'd wanted since we visited my auntie in Balerno when I was a young boy. We have had lovely neighbours in both Edinburgh and Fife so we have been lucky. We have the Driftland race car track at the end of the street, Knockhill and other parks are not far either. We have a shooting range five minutes away and we have gone kayaking for my niece's birthday. Cherise has been promised horse riding lessons. She wanted an actual horse and we had only spent one night in the house.

No sirens, no drugs, no drunks – this is my life now. Every area has their problems but nobody knows me here so I'm left in peace.

Chapter 29

The next time you go for a job interview and they ask you, 'If you were an animal which would it be?', please don't say 'sheep'. I was asked that question at an interview and no, I didn't reply 'sheep'. I replied 'tiger' – quick, powerful and solitary.

Make all the decisions in your life and take the credit when you get it right and learn from it when you don't. We all make mistakes in our lives and it's how we deal with them and learn from them that makes us who we are. Have nobody to blame for your mistakes or you won't learn jack. You will tell yourself it's their fault. You can't go through life blaming everybody else or wallowing in self-pity as it will cause depression. Everybody has different mindsets so it's just working out how yours has been working. It's taken you to where you are now and if you're not happy in this place you have the power to change. I've only recently realised this myself.

Don't be scared to follow your dreams. If you always just follow everyone else, then you are not following your own dreams. Start small and build yourself up to a point where your confidence is rising. Remember and plan for the negative people. Block the negative and keep positive. It's harder when it's people you love, but it's a good test to show yourself that talking to yourself is working. Find your own technique and when it works hold onto that forever. Use anything you can,

You need to start thinking for yourself as it's the only way to control your own life. It's not easy to start but if you believe it's possible then I promise it's much quicker. When you take a knock in life you must be in control. Be super-aware of your choices, even if people are laughing at you for following your dreams. Whatever it is you must decide to deflect the negative thoughts.

When I was wee and I couldn't sleep, my mum would come into the room and say: 'Count some sheep, then.' So I closed my eyes and visualised some sheep, then I put a fence in, then I had some sheep starting to jump the fence. Black sheep, white sheep, any colour – it didn't matter. That wee person that made that possible was my mind. I never knew that at the time but wish I had understood it more.

We can create what we are expecting to happen in our world by the way we think. If we change how we are thinking on the inside, then things around us on the outside will begin to change. The whole idea is to create the new you – the sort of person you want to be. Try thinking about what you think about you, and you will realise that there's a lot you will want to change. Make it happen!

Change the way you think about things and you can change the way you live your life. I'm still changing things in my life for the better so it's no easy fix, pardon the pun. I got angry with the person looking back at me, so get yourself a mirror and keep telling yourself that you will achieve whatever you choose, only be positive. Reject all the negative putdowns. You need to stop all the negative garbage and accept compliments. Inside, tell yourself how good and able you are. I'm living, breathing proof that it can be done, so don't doubt it for a second. Take each day at a time and never give up. The people you spend time with will never believe you can change unless you prove it. The chances are you will automatically reject a lot of the things I am saying because you won't believe you can achieve change. If I spoke to you it would make a difference, because you would realise it is achievable to get clean of drugs and start a new life without them. It's a very conscious thing when you start making changes in your head. You will notice straight away and it feels great. Keep that feeling and use it.

You're not dead until your heart stops beating. Always follow your dreams and always have a Plan B. Remember that life will always throw curveballs at you. What matters is how you deal with them. Be strong and positive and it will carry you far in your life. I still have my own issues but I don't let them define me. Keep the glass half full, not half empty. I use this a lot in my own life and it helps me a lot.

Chapter 30

I was browsing Facebook one day when I came across a post about a lad who turned his life around from drug addiction. It made me really think about my story and if it was time to tell strangers.

Three or four times in the last few years I burned almost everything I wrote. Picking up my pen again was something I waited for so long, because you really have to be in a certain frame of mind. Writing was therapy but now I only write positive words as I hope to inspire someone, anyone to kick the heroin. The manuscript of this book almost went on the fire last year, never to be published. I'm glad it didn't.

It should not matter to anyone my reasons for helping the homeless or addicts of this world. All that matters is that people are trying to help. We can make changes to this country on our own, but we really need the super-wealthy to step in and do it quickly. Needless lives lost seems to be a thing of late – the coronavirus really has shaken this country.

Money makes the world go round. For me that's the biggest and worst addiction of all. All over the globe suffering is mostly caused by lack of funds. People addicted to money are driven by greed. I noticed from an early age the gap in wealth in this country and we just accept it. It's nothing to do with who works harder, although we all know who wins that one. It's the hard-working people who suffer every single time. My whole life I've watched the rich get richer and the poor stay poor. Corruption is everywhere and it can never be abolished, but homelessness can.

We need money injected into the foundations of this country and build up, not drip down. The billions we should get somehow go missing and it's brushed aside. Anyone who questions it is most likely silenced. It all begins with a lie, just one lie can spread corruption. If you would do anything to protect your secret or your family, then maybe you make some choices that you know are wrong. I believe guilt will always drain these people. Deep down they know it's wrong to steal money but are trapped.

Without finding our own wealth as a nation we will always suffer. We have amazing resources and should all be rich. Homelessness should never be a thing. Money dictates how many get helped, but that's morally wrong so we must do it properly ourselves. We can all pull together, every single person working to their limits and it will work. Helping those worse off is a trait I've carried my whole life. Even when I had a drug addiction I would share what I had. I never wanted to be controlled by money but I needed some to live.

Everyone is capable of helping. Give a man a fish and he will feed his family for a day; give a man a rod and he will feed his family forever. Grow our own and dig out the minerals in our land to do it. Protect ourselves from the greedy and inject all the money into the homeless situation, then move onto all the other issues. Everyone can be better off financially. The rich will still get richer, but now the poor will get richer. I can see all that needs to happen and hope they will listen. Solar panels are an essential part of our heating crisis – wind and sea also, but solar can be installed quickly and saving lives next winter.

This book aims to inspire and give hope to everyone suffering that we do care about them, they have lost their way a bit but that doesn't mean we should abandon them. There will always be bad apples, but that doesn't mean we should stop helping those in need.

I love Hibs more than I hate Hearts. I want that to catch on. It's important to think about what it means. It applies to everything I'm doing at the moment. Try it now and see what you come up with. I want to watch Saturday Night Takeaway because I love Ant more than I hate Dec, for instance. Anything you can think of. The glass half full is important and all these positive vibes are best said out loud. The first reason is you listen to yourself and it feels nice. It also lets those around you know that you're being positive. It's contagious and people will be drawn to you.

Be wary of bloodsuckers, but never let them break your spirit. Nobody is bigger or better than anyone else. The wealth divide in this country causes a major unrest, and you can't blame people for being angry.

I hope to bridge a gap and inject some much-needed wealth right at the bottom. Build a foundation, an infrastructure that works, then put these people back under a roof.

Addiction is really where my time must be focused, so please if you're reading this book and you have a spare few quid then give a shout. We must stop the rot and all come under one umbrella. Charities across Scotland all combining is the only way to abolish homelessness.

Help isn't always welcome, and I have to make sure I don't waste time trying to help people who are not ready, because there are people waiting to be saved.

We don't have to get everyone off the streets, but I'd settle for everyone who wants a fresh start to get one. The rest might come round when they see how much we are helping the others. Winter is coming and no, not from Game of Thrones but to Scotland. Every year we lose people to being cold and that is disgusting. In the year 2020, with the wealth we have and the technology we have at our disposal, we can't heat our country in the winter months. Elderly people are treated horribly too and that sickens me. They have worked their whole lives (and yes, you can assume they all worked, there were no dossers back in those days) but are forgotten about and have small pensions. That is no way to treat these amazing people. I lost all my grandparents when I was young and that was hard on the family. We were young so it didn't affect us as much, but it couldn't have been easy for my parents, auntie and uncle.

There are too many people on the streets, if there's even one. I plan to get sleeping bags and food this year for them. You're reading this book so you are feeding and sheltering them. My ideas seem optimistic until you see them unfold in front of your eyes.

I wish I'd respected money more because I have a family to think about. I got a settlement for my injuries and I've literally done nothing but give it away. It's horrible to know you can help and don't. I get guilt-tripped easily and I'm very gullible at times. Of course, I have attracted the wrong sorts of people. A radar must go off or something. I need support with this side of me, but I'm happy and that's all that counts. Money eases suffering so it helps me feel better about myself. My wife helps keep me grounded or I would have nothing. Writing this book will generate money to help and I'm proud of myself for finishing it.

On finishing this book I had the exact same feeling as the day I stopped taking heroin – massive goosebumps and shivers down my spine. Only this time around I'd managed to work out everything I was doing wrong. Share, share, share!

Chapter 31

So we have come to the end of Heroin To Hero, Chapter One, and I must say that writing this book has been the most stressful thing I've ever done. I have been talking to myself for fourteen years now and I've proven you can follow your dreams, time and time again. I hope you have taken something from this book, but the purpose has always been to reach out to those in need.

If after reading this you feel a lot of what I say makes sense, then please look around your immediate family and think, 'could I help?' If not, a friend or even a stranger. The more people who read this book, the bigger chance of helping. I plan to be speaking a lot more for the people of Scotland in the future. Tackling homelessness is my first mission. I won't stop until it's done because I feel in my heart and mind that I can actually help a lot of people, even if I'm on my own.

This book and all its proceeds will go directly to the cause of homelessness in Scotland, and I plan to tackle addiction issues all over the world through educational videos. I will keep speaking until someone listens. You may have already seen the videos I've done, I can talk for hours if I'm passionate.

This book will save lives and for that reason it's worth it.

This book is also for people struggling to believe they can change. It's my pleasure to share my life with the rest of you too, of course. I have had more sad times than happy times in my life, but the happy times mean so much more that I flood my head with those. Quality over quantity.

Now things are clear I see no need to doubt myself. I have watched my videos back and as much as I cringe what I say makes perfect sense. I do rabbit on a bit, but I can see where the problems are so why not go fix them. If by selling my soul I can save one life, then I will sleep easy. I hope you have enjoyed my stories. There are plenty more, but I need to start focusing on the charity now. No time for negative thoughts.

People will always judge me but I want to help and that's what drives me. Homeless people need help, but not just food and sleeping bags. Their needs are not being met and in a wealthy nation I find it disgusting and very sad. I'm a proud Scotsman and things like this really make me feel ashamed. If I'm doing all this to make myself feel better then I can live with that. There are many issues but hopefully I can build trust around the globe and bring enough wealth to Scotland to completely abolish homelessness. I'd much rather the super-wealthy in Scotland got on board, but we need a blank cheque.

I believe in destiny. I'm still not sure what that means for Paul Boggie, but everything has aligned properly in my head. My fear is I'm too confident and too positive for those who love me. Will they still love me when my head explodes a bit? Happiness is key for us all as humans. I am still sad a lot, and angry too, but it's less than half so I'm ok. Perfect I'll never be, but I do try to be a good man and have a heart. I must make sure that I stay in control and I can only do that through talking to myself. I love Hibs more than I hate Hearts, I love Scotland more than I hate England… I'm British, too, and those are still my brothers down south or anywhere in the UK. Some Scots refer to the English as cousins or distant cousins, enemies even. But we are all on this rock together so we must always be a team. I watch Braveheart and the passion is really heartfelt, but then I watch Band of Brothers and feel the same heartfelt emotions. I've learned to take every human being at face value. If you have a big heart we will get on.

When you read my next chapter, you will see a very different Paul Boggie. Stories of hope, stories of generosity, stories of positive changes.

Goodbye

Sitting here smoking my grass joint while waiting to hear from famous Scottish people to endorse my book is stressful but my heart is in here with you. Right now I'm going to cry because I felt happy writing 'goodbye' and it wasn't a suicide note.

So, I'm still here. Drying my eyes and writing my thank you to everyone reading this book. That was not a nice place to be, but for Scotland I'll relive those memories forever. I hope you took some information or at least got to know me better. I have always known I should be doing something good. My only regret is not finishing the book sooner. In a perfect world we would all get on, but without a cloud of weed in the air that won't happen. Instead we will drink ourselves into a frenzy because we are, after all, Scottish. I don't drink because I can't be trusted not to get upset and emotional. Maybe now I'm truly happy I'll be ok, but honestly I think I need to stay as clean as possible. My back means I need pain relief, or can I find another way? We will see.

I'm bringing this book to a close now, because it's time to focus on homelessness in Scotland, then the rest of the world will see how I did it and copy me – simplified slightly but possible. It's my dream and I'm following it, and life will try to stop me but I will stay on course until homelessness is abolished.

I'm proud to say I'm originally from Leith, brought up in Craigentinny, adulthood in Lochend. I'm proud to say I'm from Edinburgh, but most of all I love being Scottish. I've nothing against the rest of Great Britain because I love you too, but I feel in my heart that I'm Scottish. When I see the Union Jack now, I see the army in my mind and that makes me happy. Hopefully I have made Britain proud.

I'm about to cry again so I'll leave you with this. Life has been a rollercoaster, but I can't regret the bad downturns because the life knowledge I've gained is priceless and I'm willing to share everything I have in my head.

All that's needed for evil to triumph is for good people to do nothing.

104

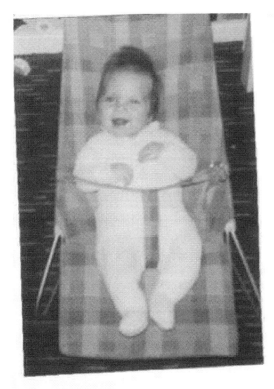

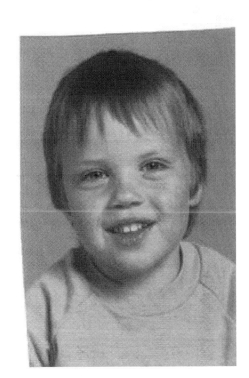

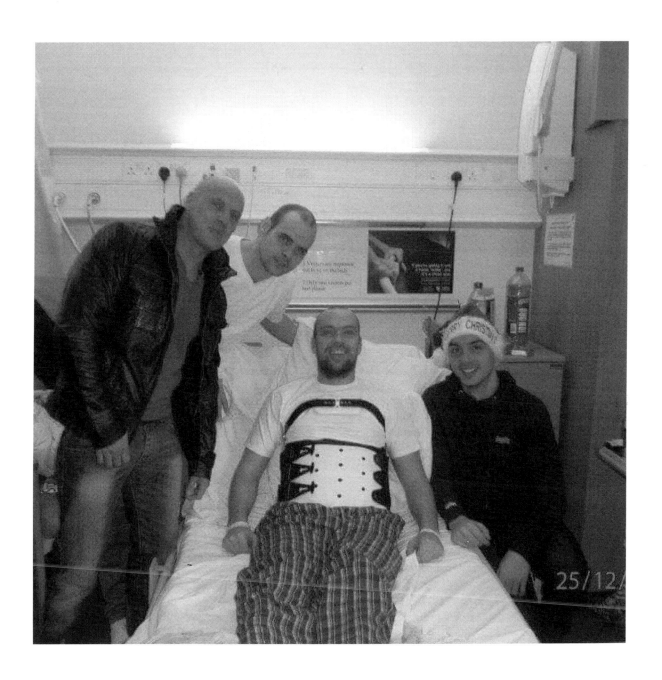

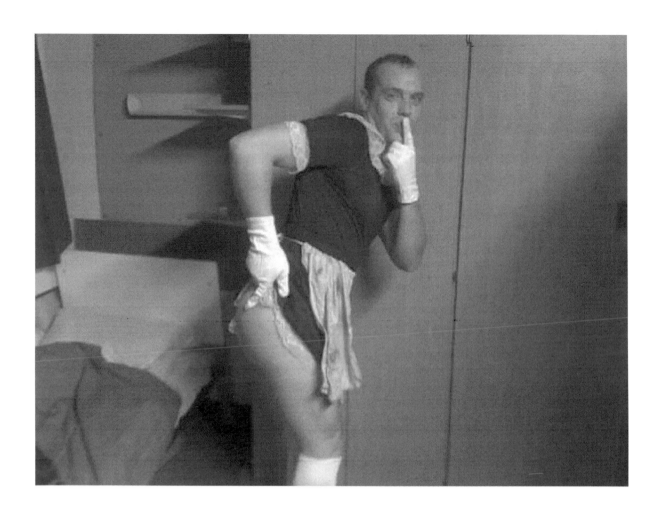

118

121

122

Printed in Great Britain
by Amazon